Praise for *Love, Fo...*

"If every person would read this [...] wisdom shared by Bill and Da[...] improved and the face of mental una emotional health would be dramatically transformed."
—Dr. Jody Stanislaw
Naturopathic Doctor, and Author, *Hunger*

"Bill is the real deal. I want my leader with battle wounds. I don't want any leaders who are polished and unscathed. That leadership ain't working. This is what leadership looks like. This is what it looks like."
—Bo Eason
NFL standout, acclaimed Broadway performer and story coach

"Daniele's determination to transform her life to what it is today, despite the hardships she has endured, is infectious. She inspires her clients, friends, and the entire diabetes community to live with strength and passion. Anyone will benefit from reading this book."
—Asha Agar Brown
Founder and Executive Director, We Are Diabetes

"We can all learn from Bill's example no matter how small or large we think our problems are... His story will change the way you look at life!"
—Priya Rana Kapoor
Author, *Give YourSelf Permission to Live Your Life*

"Bill's story is one of the most incredible examples of perseverance and inner strength there is. His ability to not only overcome, but forgive and move forward is world class."
—Brent Seal
CEO of Mavrixx, and Mountaineer

"Daniele is a consistent source of positivity, ambition, and inspiration. She's experienced struggle and she's worked her way towards success. She's shared her journey and wisdom on achieving success in many ways, and this book is the official cherry on top!"
—Ginger Vieira
Writer, Author, Editor Emeritus at Diabetes Daily

"Hearing Bill's story has altered my life in ways that I lack the vocabulary to fully express but I know I am but one of many lives he will change along his journey."
—Kip Brooks
Cofounder of Mental & Emotional Freedom

"Daniele is all about making the best of this life, no matter what health obstacles get in your way — and she does it with compassion and grace. I send folks her way all the time because I trust that her work is loaded with integrity and love."
—Jenni Grover
Blogger, Chronic Babe, Author, *Chronic Babe 101*

"Bill has an amazing, vulnerable, and heartfelt story to tell that will make you think twice about how you're approaching your life and business. He is one of the rare few individuals I know who demonstrates what it is to REALLY walk the walk."
—Michael Rozbruch
Founder, Tax and Business Solutions Academy

"Not only is Bill and Daniele's story inspiring, they live out the principles he teaches every day in their interactions with the people around them."
—Kurt Black
Founder, Automate To Liberate

"Bill is an expert life and business strategist with a big heart and contagious enthusiasm to match it with. If you follow and listen to what he has to say, you will make a bigger impact in the world, no doubt about it."
—Andy Zitzmann
Global Leader of Isilon Global Alliances & OEM, Dell EMC

"The thing with Bill and Daniele's experience is that, at its core, it's a very human story that anyone can relate to. Their story of overcoming the odds is one that is sure to inspire and motivate you to make the most out of your life."
—Ron Sparkman
Founder of Stardom

Love, Forgive, Never Give Up!

3 Powerful Ways To Turn Tragedy Into Triumph, Adversity Into Advantage, And Take Your Life To The Next Level

BILL HARGENRADER
DANIELE HARGENRADER

See the special offer after the last chapter to find out how you can read book 2 for FREE!

Sign up for book updates and free resources at
http://LFNBook.com

Philadelphia

Love, Forgive, Never Give Up! and Epic Journeys are a trademark of Epic Journeys Entertainment, LLC
Published   by   Epic   Journeys   Entertainment
PO Box 14596 | Philadelphia, PA 19115

ISBN: 0692126619
ISBN-13: 978-0692126615

Dedicated to everyone who could use a light to illuminate their next step through the dark...

And to those who are ready to shine their light even brighter, so others may see more clearly.

TABLE OF CONTENTS

"With everything that has happened to you, you can either feel sorry for yourself or treat what has happened as a gift. Everything is either an opportunity to grow or an obstacle to keep you from growing. You get to choose."

— Wayne Dyer

AUTHORS' NOTE

Note to self: This is going to hurt. This is going to hurt a lot.

That's the note I wrote to myself one day before I revisited a painful experience in my life in order to write this book.

When setting out to write a self-help book on overcoming adversity, tragedy, struggle, and suffering, we must be possessed of great courage.

Daniele and I have passed through some trying times and emerged victorious—or in some situations, at a minimum, we survived and that counts as a win in our book (both figuratively and literally).

To retell a story from your past in a way that is meaningful and impactful means actually reliving that experience. Going there in our hearts, minds, and bodies and experiencing the emotions and thoughts, the joys and pains, the good and the bad. And the bad hurts.

Part of what Daniele and I teach is to live in the present—in the now. Now is the only time you have real power. We want to use stories of the past and our experiences to empower us, but hurtful experiences rarely empower us unless we actively give them the right meaning. There is an exception to this rule: if you can retell and relive your experience in order to help another avoid or overcome their own struggles, then that is a worthy and ultimately empowering reason to go there.

This book is really about choosing the meaning you want to make with your life—how you want to feel and how you want to make others feel—then consciously choosing your actions and aligning them with living in creating that meaning.

My purpose now is to be a healthy, wealthy, loving, joyful, powerful, phenomenal role model leader of leaders, to enjoy living, learning, growth and progress, to grow my positive energy, mission and vision, and to share it with others so we can massively change the world for the better together.

Daniele's purpose is to embody love—to be love. At a seminar we attended in 2009, we were prompted to come up with a purpose statement for our lives. It was a difficult task, and Daniele struggled hard with that exercise. This is what she came up with after an hour of thinking, crying, and deep-feeling:

The purpose of my life is to be a force of love, to enjoy giving and receiving love, and to take care of the Earth and all of its inhabitants by being loving.

Back then, she said she had no idea where the words came from; they just ended up on the paper. Today, it is crystal clear to both of us that those words came from her source energy of love even before she knew the true power of consciously and intentionally embodying love.

We tie all of our actions back to that purpose, or at least have conditioned our awareness to do so the very vast majority of the time. My purpose will evolve in the future, and one thing is for sure, it was not always what it is today.

Thirty years ago, something happened to me that would change my life forever. At just 8 years old, my purpose became to simply survive, to figure out how to solve the puzzle of being wrongfully imprisoned, and to be strong enough to suffer through the darkness long enough so that someday I would wake up and things would be better.

Your current purpose may be anywhere on the spectrum from survive to thrive—from barely living to contributing and giving. Or you may not have ever thought about your purpose, and that's okay too. If you haven't considered your purpose yet, I suggest simply making your purpose: to improve my life and the lives of others and to discover and create my true purpose.

Love, Forgive, Never Give Up! gives you a framework that is designed to stand on its own or fit within your own chosen lifestyle and purpose. The tools and strategies we provide will be even more powerful when combined with your own internally inspired purpose.

When you have purpose—any purpose—you can endure. You can survive. You can make it to the next day. And if you can make it to the next day and have a mindset of continually improving, then someday things will feel better. Either your situation will change or your mindset will change about your situation. Either way, it will get better.

If you're already doing great right now, then by adding a little more love and forgiveness to your life and knowing that your story of perseverance has the ability to inspire and help others get through their trying times, life can become even more fulfilling.

When we raise our hands, when we tell our stories, when we shine our light, there are others in the dark who, for the first time, will be able to see a path forward, up and out. When we reach our current goals or when we are feeling stuck, when we experience personal success or failure, and when we scale our highest peaks or slide down the side of the mountain, that is always the right time to reach back with a helping hand to help someone else up.

Shine your light brightly, love strong, be forgiving, and never, ever give up.

—Bill and Daniele Hargenrader
Philadelphia, PA 17MAY2018

OUR
STORIES

YOUR STORY PART I

I am the master of my fate,
I am the captain of my soul.
From the poem "Invictus" by William Ernest Henley

Throughout the pages of this book we will tell you our stories, but this book is really about *your* story.

Because ultimately, it's always up to you to decide what your life story is going to be about.

We are continually writing the stories of our lives through our actions, and it's up to us to determine the meaning our lives have in every moment—day to day, year to year—for our entire lives.

There is certainly a heavy weight of responsibility in that idea. Of course, we all know that we are responsible for our own actions. However, remaining unaware of or denying the role you play in authoring the story of your own life is akin to being tossed about like a raft at the whims of the ocean and the wind.

Occasionally it will be beautiful and peaceful on your raft, with the sun's rays glistening off the mists of the waves as whales and dolphins dance upon the water.

And other days (likely more often than not), your raft will be drenched and tossed about in the storms of the sea of life, nearly capsized at every moment by massive rising waves, while the darkened skies hurl lightning and sound thunderous doom.

To be sure, even when you decide to take charge of your life—taking on the role of author and protagonist—you will still face both sunny days and stormy ones. The difference is that you won't be riding helplessly on a raft. Instead, you will command a sailboat that harnesses the winds of life and guides you toward your destination through pleasant and rough seas alike.

As you read the stories that Daniele and I tell, we encourage you to reflect back upon how you can apply the information and lessons in your own life, and to the situations and circumstances in it.

We aren't motivated to tell the tales of our darkest moments and how we fought through immense suffering just to earn your admiration, attention, or any other accolades. We tell these tales in hopes of having the privilege and honor of inspiring you to see a hint of a path forward in your life that you may not have seen before—to provide the spark that will light the fire of hope and courage in you.

You'll see many more "Your Story" sections throughout this book. Use these sections wisely to integrate what you have learned. After all, this book is nothing if not used by you to help yourself and others.

And remember, you are the master of your fate. You are the captain of your soul.

You are living the story of your life whether you've been authoring it consciously or unconsciously. And more than that, you are now living your Next Level Life Story.

Your Next Level Life Story is your epic tale of you overcoming the odds, using your perceived adversities to your advantage, and emerging stronger than you ever thought possible.

BILL'S STORY

THEN

I am 34 years old, the year is 2014, and my back aches as I hunch over in a darkened and crowded storage space under the stairs in the basement. I'm attempting to declutter the mess that's been building there for years, and *hopefully* make my wife, Daniele, happy in the process.

I let out a cough as the dust from the boxes of books, knickknacks, and old Army gear settles in my lungs. My hands reach out to open a tattered, unlabeled cardboard box previously buried under a pile of nondescript boxes just like it. But this box is different. My breath catches in my throat as I begin to realize what it contains.

A chill runs down my spine. An eerie sense of déjà vu overcomes me all at once. I feel rising anticipation in my mind and a sense of deepening dread in the pit of my stomach as my fingers pause in their work of revealing the contents.

Silence surrounds me. I am all alone down here. I know, without knowing how I know, that if I open this box, there is no turning back.

I need very little time to make a decision. I don't want to turn back. It's time.

I open the box fully and reach down to pick up the object resting at the top.

My heartbeat quickens and pounds in my chest like a drum. My mind races and my eyes squint in the low light to make out the words scrawled in black ink atop the crinkled, white legal pad journal in my hands:

CHRONICLES
OF THE
WARRIOR LOST.

I am all that is left of an experiment gone wrong. The rest has been destroyed. It's as though I never existed. But I do exist. My name is William.

I find myself filling with a growing sense of awe as I read those words of half-truths from my 13-year-old self, 21 years prior. The words are those of a boy with an active imagination, but the flood of emotions and memories that race through my mind feel very real. The false imprisonment in the mental institution. The years of living a lie, unable to speak my truth. The twisted struggle to find my humanity. The seemingly impossible battle for my very sanity. And the long journey towards forgiveness and healing with my family.

The words on the legal pad are a statement of purpose for the boy who wrote them all those years ago. For my adult self, they are a time portal to my youth. They are a hidden message that, if decoded, may lead me to some unknown revelation.

The notebooks that fill this box are like jumbled pieces of a puzzle—a puzzle that may lead to further healing for me and my family, and maybe even help others that might be going through tough times. I like puzzles. I'm good at puzzles. I get the rising sense I know I can figure this one out if I put my mind to it.

Excited now, intent on unraveling the mystery I laid out for myself as a boy, I step out of the dark storage space into the light of the basement and squat down on my haunches, ready to begin the story.

NOW

That experience years ago, finding my short stories and journals under the stairs, set me off on a course of action I did not expect and led directly to writing this book, which you are reading right now.

I'll revisit passages from the *Chronicles of the Warrior Lost* throughout this book, but for now, the big takeaway is that there is immense power in reviewing your life story and creating a positive meaning from what you've been through.

For me, when I was 8 years old, something happened that would change the course of my life forever. I was sent to a mental institution for 3 years for a crime I didn't commit. And yet, that painful experience ultimately became the source of my greatest strength.

Though it took a very long time to figure that out.

This book's aim is to help you get through your own struggles much faster and realize your greatest strengths in good times and bad.

I only had a fleeting hope that it was possible at the time, but through my own experience and through studying those that have mastered turning adversity into advantage, a pattern began to emerge.

A framework of feelings and emotions that, if held in the forefront of my mind, made the biggest difference in achieving the life I knew in my heart of hearts was possible.

What I have discovered is that the three most powerful guiding forces that helped me and countless others find their path and gain their footing in life are:

- Love
- Forgiveness
- Never giving up

For me, it took a massive tragedy, pain, and suffering to discover these forces.

It all started one fateful night when one of my six brothers set fire to our house. No one got hurt, but I got the blame, and I was sent away to a mental institution.

I still remember my first night in that padded cell. Most people picture sterile, white padded walls, but it was really padded with floor-to-ceiling dirt-brown carpeting that smelled of mildew. My only glimpse of the outside world was when the nurses and doctors came to look down at me through the wire mesh window set in the door to check off the checkboxes on their clipboards.

The more I protested and professed my innocence, the sicker and more delusional the doctors said I was. I cried out to God and wondered why I had been left to suffer. I soon realized that no one was coming to save me.

I was all alone.

OUR GREATEST STRENGTH FROM OUR DARKEST MOMENTS

Yet, in that moment of complete hopelessness, I found a spark of hope.

In that moment I knew it was up to me and me alone to figure this out. I soon discovered that there is power in taking responsibility for your situation, whether it's your fault or not.

Eventually, I was able to figure out a way to gain my freedom, and years later, the truth came out. My brother confessed and my parents were devastated. They had been doing what they thought was right, but by tragic mistake sent the wrong child away. Through forgiveness, we eventually were able to come together and heal.

It would be years later yet until I was able to reconcile the dark wounds inside me and realize that I was a good person, able to love others, and worthy of being loved.

When that happened, I was able to find my perfect partner in life, Daniele. Her strength and dedication to helping others inspires me every single day, and I am grateful that we are co-authoring this book together.

Throughout all the trials and tragedies of life, with love, forgiveness, perseverance, willpower, and faith, I've been able to go from a kid locked away in a dark cell for a crime he didn't commit to becoming a US Fortune 500 expert in innovation and project management and having the privilege of leading a successful cybersecurity program for a critical $36 billion global organization.

I went from someone whose voice went unheard to becoming someone who travels the world as an international speaker, sharing my story and spreading my message to those who need to hear it.

I went from someone whose only hope in life came from reading self-help books, to becoming a bestselling author with the amazing opportunity to help others find and realize their greatest strength by writing a self-help book of my own.

It's a true honor to type these words and to know you are reading them—to know my experience can help someone else.

What I went through was painful, difficult, dark, scary… and lonely.

But I was able to realize my greatest strengths from my darkest moments. And the culmination of that strength is embedded in the lessons in this book on love, forgiveness, and never giving up.

Now I'm old enough to see the past patterns of evolution for what they are, and this book is my way of passing on some of the lessons and *practices* that helped me overcome seemingly insurmountable obstacles.

Our situations are unique to us, but the emotions we feel are shared by all of humanity.

If you're reading this book, then you know what struggle and suffering feels like. There is comfort and power in knowing that we have the shared experience of being alive, and that through telling the stories of our own struggles and relaying the solutions that worked for us, we can grow as individuals— as communities, as a society, and as a species.

You can begin to choose new stories that inspire you instead of listening to the same old story in your head telling you you're not worthy or not good enough.

You can begin to select empowering emotions that you want to feel on an ongoing basis and rewire yourself to not only make the most out of challenging situations but help others along the way.

And now, it's time for some questions: Why are you here? Why are you reading this?

You might feel that you are called to serve a higher purpose; that you are meant for more. But then you look around and see that your circumstances don't match up with your vision.

You might be in pain, going through depression, grieving for the loss of a loved one, or even thinking of ending it all.

You might be reading this because you are doing everything in your power to help someone dear to you.

Or you might not know why you are here, but you feel compelled to change things up until you discover and create the life you have always dreamed of.

You're here because you're the hero of your own story, regardless of whether or not you have ever thought of yourself as such.

You're the hero of your story who is just now realizing that it's time to take further action on your personal quest in life.

All heroes go through great struggles and emerge forever changed, and they share what they have learned with others, making their lives better as well.

Heroes in every story have to make a choice, and they always make a choice to go to the next step. They might not always know why they are moving forward or how they will do it, but they always decide to move forward anyway.

So, if you're ready to embark on the next leg of your own personal journey through life, then you have to make a decision.

Will you decide to turn back?

Or will you decide to take the next step, turn the page, and read on?

DANIELE'S STORY

When I was nine years old, I was diagnosed with an incurable autoimmune disease. My body effectively turned on itself suddenly and unexpectedly for no explainable reason. This is a disease that would guarantee my certain death within a few weeks' time if not carefully monitored and attended to in some way almost constantly—day and night, twenty-four hours a day, seven days a week, 365 days a year, with no breaks or time off. Ever.

What disease could this be, you may be wondering? You've likely heard of it a million times before on TV, in the doctor's office, from people you know, and, sadly, probably in a joking manner.

In addition to requiring the vigilance and level of attention described above just to remain alive, it is the only disease I've ever heard of that is so widely accepted as the butt of countless, unending jokes from all manner of human population, including medical professionals. But unless you live with this disease yourself, or in the same home as someone who lives with it, you cannot truly understand what this disease is or all that is required of the person living with it (physically, emotionally, and spiritually) to simply stay alive, let alone remain healthy and seemingly "normal."

This disease is called type 1 diabetes.

It began with extreme, unquenchable thirst, incessant urination, frequent stomachaches, and losing weight no matter how much I ate. In September of 1991, a quick diagnosis at the doctor's office facilitated by a simple finger prick blood glucose test led to my immediate admittance to the hospital, where I stayed for seven days. My mom slept on a cot next to my hospital bed, never leaving my side. My dad did his best to hold down the plumbing business they co-owned while trying to comfort me and my mom and process everything that was happening.

Information was dumped on us in a cold, systematic, almost robotic manner, filled with doom, gloom, fear, and the promise of a life that seemed guaranteed to be filled with diabetes-related complications. Even though many of the words they used didn't make much sense to me as a nine-year-old, the impact they had on my mindset as I grew older and began to understand them turned out to be hugely impactful after all, in a myriad of negative ways.

At the time, all I knew was that my parents didn't *seem* to be that scared. Other than needing to inject myself with insulin every single time I ate or drank or my blood sugar was out of range, and checking my blood glucose levels sometimes up to twelve times a day with seemingly endless finger pricks with a sharp little lancet, life went on.

I went back to school. I grew as used to needles and visits to the nurse's office several times a day to check my blood glucose and eat snacks as a nine-year-old could. I grew accustomed to the odd looks and questions from the other kids. "Why do *you* get to go eat snacks whenever you want? You're so lucky!"

My parents always had the attitude that whatever came our way, we would figure it out. I trusted in that outlook and their ever-present love and care.

And for a few years, it worked. Until it didn't.

SOMETIMES IT GETS WORSE BEFORE IT GETS BETTER

My father died suddenly three years after my diagnosis, the day after my twelfth birthday.

I am certain he held on until after midnight just so my birthday and the day of his death wouldn't fall on the same date for the rest of my life. He died shortly after midnight on August 25, 1994.

The constant needs involved with living with type 1 diabetes, plus the knowledge that there was (and still is) no cure, combined with the life-altering death of my father and puberty-ridden hormones led me into a veritable tailspin of physical and emotional fallout. By the time I was fourteen, I weighed over 200 pounds and was diagnosed as clinically depressed. I was prescribed antidepressants and my willingness to care for or about myself had completely disappeared.

My classmates' comments about how "lucky" I was to get to go the nurse's office and eat snacks soon changed, taking on a painful callousness born of ignorance and lack of empathy.

Now that I was much heavier (and taller) than the majority of the other kids my age, the comments turned dark and ugly. "No wonder you're so fat, always going to eat snacks and drink juice all day." "Maybe if you didn't leave class to eat so much, you wouldn't be so fat." One of the kids even gave me a nickname: "The Fridge."

The same nickname of a 350-pound football player on our home team. The pain and shame the bullying caused me at the time was indescribable, the fear of knowing that he would continue to call me that in front of other people crippled me as a young teenager.

The weighing 200 pounds aspect of this reality came from my newly-found binge-eating addiction. With my father gone, my mom had to work full-time at a new job in order to take care of us and to ensure we had the health insurance I needed to stay alive.

Since I was always very mature for my age, I took two buses home from school every day in the big city of Philadelphia. What my mom didn't know was that almost every day, I would stop off at the store to buy junk food before getting home. The nastiest, most heavily processed, and damaging foods were (and still are) the cheapest to buy.

I would eat inordinate amounts of junk food while my mom was still at work and then hide the rest of it in my room and wait until she went to bed to eat more. To say this was a vicious, emotionally, physically, and spiritually painful cycle would be an understatement.

Binge eating both comforted me and at the same time fueled my hatred for myself and my diabetes. I had no idea how to—or if I was ever going to—find my way out of this reality.

Thanks to the loving encouragement of my dad, I always trusted in the awesome power of my brain, in the fact that I was (and am) smart, and that if I did not know the answer to something, I could figure it out if I tried. When I brought my first report card home from first grade, he gave me five dollars for every A I earned, and no monetary reward for any other grades. So, at six years old, I equated being smart and applying yourself when learning to financial gain. I am eternally grateful for that lesson.

Thanks to that incredibly valuable lesson, I eventually decided I was going to learn my way out of my circumstances.

I finally felt in my heart and soul while looking in the mirror one day that the person looking back at me wasn't the real *me*. I knew the real *me* was in there, hidden under many layers of fear and pain, and I finally figured out that I was and would always be the only person who could begin choosing new, different actions to face those fears and heal that pain.

I decided to get my bachelor's degree in Nutrition Science. I also decided to go to personal training school (even though at the time I couldn't do a single push-up, was still overweight, and had, only a few months prior, began inconsistently dabbling in weightlifting). I spent 500 hours over six months learning detailed information about human anatomy and physiology and how to put that knowledge into *practice*.

I skeptically decided to attend a Tony Robbins seminar, knowing that if I came away with just *one* new idea, perspective, or proven system of organizing my mindset in a more productive pattern, my time and money would not be wasted. I came away with *so much* more than that.

I searched for mentors—for people who were living their lives to the fullest, both despite and *because* of having experienced extreme adversity. I constantly read about people's fat-loss journeys and the variety of ways so many different people blazed their trail to feeling healthy in their own skin. I began incessantly seeking out ways that others had turned adversity into advantage, tragedy into triumph, both for themselves and for others.

And that was just the beginning.

THE SUPERHERO INSIDE

Interestingly enough, one of my major influences in my formative years was Dwayne Johnson, also known as The Rock. I began watching WWE wrestling around the age of fourteen. It become a weekly tradition—Monday Night Raw and Thursday Night SmackDown were televised events that my best friends and I would get together and watch. We even went to several live events with homemade posters and all. It was effectively a soap opera with half-naked men, and apparently, that's what I was into!

When I started watching, Johnson wasn't the mega movie star he has grown into today. I was just immediately and intensely drawn to his character (both real and "fake"). He was almost always one of the "good guys," yet he took no crap. The other thing that got my attention was his physical transformation. He wasn't always ripped, and at some points was even a little pudgy. Something about his energy just drew me in, and those who have known me my whole life will attest to me being one of his longest-standing fans.

I attribute some of my becoming known in the diabetes space as the Diabetes Dominator to the badass yet loving strength I learned from watching The Rock. Bill and I chose the Diabetes Dominator superhero persona to help me grow into the person I wanted to be well before it was ever the name of my successful coaching business, book, and more.

The Diabetes Dominator mindset has allowed me to reach and help over a million people—with and without diabetes—to love themselves more deeply by learning how to find joy in caring for their total health, mind, body, and spirit.

I could definitely smell what The Rock was cooking!

WE GET TO CHOOSE

Throughout all these experiences, I was able to explore and *consciously decide* who I believed I was, what I valued, and how to handle my feelings and emotions in consistently healthy, sustainable ways, all stemming from self-love and self-care. I learned that love (particularly self-love) was the biggest and most important missing link, and I learned how to always love myself for who I am, no matter the inevitable changes that life consists of. I eventually realized that guiding myself and others along this path of self-discovery through love and the power of choice was my purpose in life—my dharma.

Intuitively, I knew if I could make such drastic and long-lasting changes in my own mental, physical, and spiritual health, I had to do whatever I could to facilitate that journey to learning how to feel healthy and happy—regardless of circumstance—for others.

Throughout the ongoing healing process, I became conscious and present. I stopped re-living the past and worrying about the future. I woke the hell up.

I consciously forgave myself for the way I had treated my mind, body, and spirit. I forgave myself for the binging and the horrible things I used to say to myself, and I let go of any blame I had placed on myself for having diabetes or for my dad dying. Diabetes was not my fault, but it was certainly my responsibility and until there is a cure, it always will be.

Giving up was never an option for me. Even in my darkest, most self-loathing times, I never wanted my life to cease. The thought did enter my mind on more than one occasion, especially while on antidepressants, but whatever energy or force that was always present in me somehow dismissed the idea as quickly as it entered.

Perseverance, I believe, is in my blood, my bones, my cells, my DNA, and my spirit, not because I'm unique, but because I'm *human* (and if you're reading this book, I'll bet you are too). Even when things seemed unhealable and felt like they would never get better, I still kept moving toward a light I trusted was there, even though at the time I was a self-proclaimed atheist (I've since shed that label).

Sometimes I could see the light clearly. Other times I could only catch a glimpse. And sometimes I couldn't see it at all in the surrounding darkness. Eventually, I realized it was me who was in control of how brightly that light was shining—that I was the light—that I am the light.

I have gone from a fearful girl with a chronic disease who lost her father, whose physical, emotional, and spiritual health spiraled out of control for many years to becoming a loving, grateful, joyful, empathetic, confident, empowered woman. A wife to the most incredible life partner I ever could have dreamed of, a successful entrepreneur that gets to truly love my work every day, diabetes coach, life coach, bestselling author, keynote speaker, connector, consultant, and most importantly, a happy and healthy human that knows my internal wisdom and intuition will always be the most valuable assets I will ever have that no person or thing can ever take away.

I went from my sole focus being learning how to help myself become the person I wanted to be, utilizing the knowledge I put into action and shaping these steps into proven, repeatable systems, to teaching others how to do the same for themselves. I had to, and I must continue to do so—I truly feel *called*.

In teaching others the intuitive and life-long process of love, forgiveness, interrupting old patterns and reconditioning new ones, learning, growth, and contribution via mindful and present self-love *practices*, I get to continually learn, grow, and contribute personally. It is a beautifully fulfilling and fruitful cycle.

I didn't have the self-awareness tools back then to understand that the unconsciously conditioned questions I kept asking myself were contributing to my depression and overall negatively charged mindset. I was presupposing that I had done something wrong—everything wrong—when in reality the only thing I was doing wrong was blaming myself for circumstances beyond my control and not taking responsibility for the circumstances that were in my control.

I now know that the only thing I and all other humans can control are the choices we make, and our choices are the most powerful things to be in control of as they determine our reality every second of every day.

I implore you to *choose* to let love, forgiveness, and perseverance lead the way for you in *all* your decision-making processes—from what to have for breakfast to who to spend your time with, to everything in between and beyond. It's not easy at first, and it takes a lot of *practice*, but nothing radically life-improving is ever easy. I promise that it is worth every single second—inevitable setbacks and failures included. Every setback is a setup for a comeback.

The only thing in this life that you can control with any level of certainty or consistency are your choices, and in the words of Tony Robbins, "It is in your moments of decision that your destiny is shaped."

So I ask you now, and will continue to ask again and again and again... What will you choose?

YOUR STORY PART 2

"Growth is painful. Change is painful. But nothing is as painful as staying stuck somewhere you don't belong."
—Mandy Hale

What lessons have you learned? What thoughts on your story—your *Next Level Life*—have started coming up?

You could take the time to retrace your steps, to go back to the point in your life that you began to believe you were not worthy of love or forgiveness from yourself or others—or even that you were unlovable or unforgivable or unable to love or forgive others.

This would be a valuable and worthwhile exercise only if you are willing to learn from it and remain present, knowing that you are exploring a path of healing old wounds, versus judging the experience(s), participants, and yourself. Knowing where it all started can be helpful in the healing process of living into your wholeness, however, reliving the experience over and over again with no plan to break the pattern is not.

Progress is *never* linear—it is guaranteed to be studded with stumbles, falls, fails, and sometimes full-on reversions back to our old, self-destructive ways. These experiences are simply growing pains. Growing pains are very real and unavoidable, not just some cliché term or name of an old TV show.

Growing can be (and almost always is) very uncomfortable. Embracing the rough patches instead of unconsciously reverting back to your old, default numbing techniques (that we all have) is essential. Focusing on the bounce-back is everything.

Embrace the pain—*It means you're growing.* Massive shifts and breakthroughs come from growing pains. It's critical to keep in mind that if you want to evolve, you cannot avoid failure—not failing means not trying.

And let's face it, failure stings a bit, but making progress and growing as a human being is completely impossible without failing!

What's most important is that you choose to remain conscious and present enough to course correct back toward love and forgiveness more quickly each time (your bounce-back). The goal is to spend less time in the gutter than you did before as you continue down the path of healing and progress toward feeling like you are a whole, complete person—not to try to avoid failure altogether, which inevitably causes you to do nothing based solely on fear.

You must also resign to never give up on yourself as you vulnerably work towards becoming your best self and focus on the best outcomes for you, your family, friends, and those in your growing circle of influence.

We can't live our lives cowering because our efforts might not turn out the way we expected if we want to grow to help ourselves and others. Instead, we must live our lives with courage and with optimism (some might call that faith) that things will work out, that the struggles we are going through are the same struggles that the heroes in our lives and in our favorite books, TV shows, and movies must go through to grow and accomplish their missions.

Instead of focusing on failure, *practice* focusing on all of the good things that could come of your efforts. What if I get stronger and smarter? What if I help more people feel cared for? What if I feel good? What if I put all my focus on love, forgiveness, and never giving up and that fills my life with more joy than I ever thought imaginable?

Those are the pertinent questions to ask that give us courage to move forward instead of keeping us stuck in fear based inaction.

HERO'S QUEST

Will you answer the call of the Hero's Quest?

We've always enjoyed reading books and watching movies and shows like *The Princess Bride*, *The Lion King*, *The Lord of the Rings*, and *Game of Thrones* where there is an important quest to be undertaken, often by an unlikely hero.

That's why we've added in Hero's Quest sections throughout this book. Fun little snippets of adventure that help anchor in the overall flow of the book. They're short sections, so if you like them, read them, and if you don't, then feel free to skip. It's entirely up to you.

Side note: I (Daniele) was hesitant to add these sections at first, but the more the book came together, the more I jumped on board as I felt the excitement in myself rising when reading them. Plus, as someone who has adopted the moniker "Diabetes Dominator," I realize that the superhero in me has apparently spoken for itself!

HERO'S QUEST BEGINNING

You are called to a quest. A magical tome has made its way to your hands… this very book. It's perfect timing, too, because whether you know it or not, you need the information inside this book to triumph over the dark forces pervading the land and the planes of your mind.

You are the hero of your story. While you must remain open to accepting help, you also have to realize that, ultimately, you are the one who is going to save yourself.

You stop reading momentarily as the image of a treasure map appears in your mind's eye. This map shows a path to valuable artifacts and treasures, though it leads through challenging territory along the way.

You notice a feeling of strength, conviction, and confidence come over you as your eyes read these very words on the page. It seems as if the book is passing its power on to you—your mind is beginning to open to greater possibilities.

What's the first prize to be won on this quest?

It begins with a first step, and answering this riddle:

The more of me you give to yourself, the far greater your feeling of wealth.

The more of me you give away, the greater you brighten another's day.

When someone is down, I can lift them up above.

What am I? Turn the page and know that I am:

LOVE

BILL'S STORY: LOVE

THEN

My name is Billy, I am 8 years old, and I have just been inprocessed at a mental institution for a crime I didn't commit—a house fire I didn't set while I and my family slept. No one believes that I didn't do it. Not my mom, dad, firefighters, cops, or doctors. No one.

I am in the mental institution now being led down a long hallway with doors lined up on either side. And even though there are sterile fluorescent lights brightly shining down from above, I know I am being led to a very dark place. A padded cell.

My padded cell.

Two strong, stern-faced men wearing blue scrubs keep stride to my left and right as their powerful hands clamp into the flesh of my arms ushering me forward. They are possessed of a strength that seemingly nobody, let alone a small boy, could stand against.

But my attention is not on them. My focus is on the door that looms larger and larger in my vision as we approach it. My thoughts are racing and frantic—and I am very much afraid of what lies in wait for me on the other side.

We pass by another door to my left. This one is open. I hear the banshee-like screams of a woman growing louder from within. I cock my head and lean past my guards to sneak a peek inside.

I wish I hadn't.

The screaming woman's hair is bedraggled and strewn across her face. We make eye contact ever so briefly as her body is being forced down onto a bed by three men, one with his knee on her chest. Leather shackles are on her feet. One wrist is bound, and the three men are struggling to get her second lashed in.

My heart races even harder. My feet begin to stutter step as we approach my door.

"No, no, no. It wasn't me!" I shout.

I look up into those expressionless faces—the faces of men who have a job to do and do not care what I did or did not do. Besides, to them, I'm clearly guilty. To them I obviously set fire to my family's house while they slept, because I was here now. I was crazy, right? Why should they believe me?

Finally, we're at the door.

"No!" I shout again. "I didn't start the fire! It wasn't me!"

Again, no response save for the key ring attached to a swivel chain being extended toward the keyhole. And then I look up with dread in the pit of my stomach, despair in my heart, and tears in my eyes. The door swings open to reveal my new home.

I am led in roughly now, and my instincts to fight and flee kick in. I lash out screaming, "No! No! Please, God, no! Don't do this to me. It wasn't me!"

Iron-strong hands grip my arms more tightly, and I am lifted and shoved in. I barely have time to turn and see the door slam shut. I run to it and crash my body against it. Tears stream down my face.

"Please!"

I shout and shout. No one comes.

"Let me out!"

No one answers.

I slump down with my back to the door, bury my face in my hands, and cry.

"Why don't you believe me?!" I shout again as I throw my head back, cracking it hard against the door.

And with those words and the jolt from the blow, something snaps in me. Despair turns to anger, dread to rage. Tears burn hot on my face as my expression twists into a snarl.

I lift my head to look around my new environment, a fifteen-foot by fifteen-foot padded room. But it isn't white, padded walls like in the movies. Oh, no. It's a dirt-brown rug from floor to ceiling. The smell of mildew permeates the air. A lone mattress sits in the corner with no frame, lest I try to hurt myself on it. A punching bag lies on its side in the center of the floor for angry patients to hit, I suppose.

Well, I am angry.

I approach the bag, angry at my helplessness. I kick it, angry at the betrayal by one of my brothers. But which one was it? I punch down on the bag, angry at myself for letting myself get put in here. I jump on top of it and swing again, angry at my mom and dad for sending me here. I swing left and right, angry at the world for being such a cruel place.

Spit flies from my mouth, snot forms at my nose, and tears fall from my eyes as I punch and punch and punch, angry at God for doing this to me. Blind, white-hot rage flows through me.

I punch until the skin on my knuckles grows red and bloody. I punch until I am too exhausted to punch anymore.

I collapse on top of that punching bag, and my eyes go to the wire mesh window on the door where I see a nurse looking in at me, checking off boxes on an unseen clipboard. I look at her with pure hatred that comes from a deep, dark place in me—a place so deep and foreign and unknown that I didn't even know it was there. From that place of darkness come the thoughts that I say aloud.

"God," I say, "if you don't get me out of here, if you don't make all of this go away, I won't believe in you. I will know that I am all alone."

With that, I close my eyes, lay my head down on the punching bag, and drift off to a deep sleep born of exhaustion.

The next day, my eyes open in the real world.

I hope beyond hope that I'm not where I was last night. That this was all a dream within a dream, and I'll wake up for real now.

My heart sinks and my hope fades as I look around my new home. Same dirt-brown padded cell. Same smell of mildew. Same wire mesh window. My face sticks to the punching bag, and I peel my skin off its plastic surface as I sit up.

I now know beyond a shadow of a doubt that God is not coming to save me. No one is coming to save me. I brace myself for tears... But they never come. The realization that no one is coming for me should be sending me down a deeper hole of depression. Instead, to my surprise, it steels me. It gives me strength.

Why? I think, my face scrunched up in deep thought. If no one is coming to save me, then it is up to me to save myself.

Upon this realization, I sit up straight.

This is a puzzle.

My eyes grow wide with excitement.

I'm good at solving puzzles!

This is like an episode of *G.I. Joe.* I'm Snake Eyes trapped by Storm Shadow and I must find a way to overcome my foe and still save the day.

A grin creeps across my face because I know that no matter how bad this situation is, it's up to me to figure this out. I will gain my freedom. I will prove my innocence. I will get back to my family. I will make things better.

I am going to figure this out.

***

That was darkest time in my life, even as my 38-year-old self recalls it now with shivers and shudders and, yes, some tears.

And I am still emboldened by the strength we can find in our darkest times.

Immediately, my 8-year-old self became emboldened by the realization that no one was coming to save me, and now it was time to go to work on saving myself.

Fear was replaced by courage as this puzzle, this challenge, presented itself for me to solve. I imagined how one of my heroes would handle this situation. What would Luke Skywalker do? He'd use the Force, of course!

I tried to use the Force. Really tried. That didn't work.

Out of frustration, I screamed and banged on the door and shouted, "It wasn't me! It wasn't me!"

I quickly learned that just made me look crazy, so I stopped that.

After many failed attempts, I hatched a new plan. Telling the truth hadn't gotten me anywhere. In fact, the more I said it wasn't me, the more they said I was being resistant. So I figured that if I lied and admitted to setting the fire, then the doctors might think I was coming to my senses.

So I wore a *dark mask of deception*, one of my first acting roles, pretending to be mentally disturbed and wanting to get better.

And to my surprise, it worked!

The doctors deemed me on the mend, and a long 11 months later, I was declared cured.

I returned home to my family and to what I thought would be my happy ending...

But just 1 month later, one of my brothers set fire to the house again.

This time I went away for 2 full years.

***

The second time I was sent away, I protested even more vehemently that it wasn't me, but the look on the doctors' faces told me my fate was sealed. They prescribed me medication and took blood from me twice a week. I hated them sticking their needles in me, being their pincushion—I hated it so much.

When the doctors and nurses came to draw blood, they would hold me down as they jammed their needles in my arms, and forcibly took my blood while I screamed. I would hide from them under my bed, in the closet, under my desk. But they would always find me.

Finally, I made a deal with my psychiatrist. Once again, in an attempt to gain my freedom, I wore the dark mask of deception. I admitted to setting the fire. I made up some story about being jealous of my parents going out and wanting negative attention, even though in my mind I shouted, "*Who wants negative attention like that?!*"

She smiled and reduced my medication and the blood draws and told me I was getting better.

It felt like a horrible betrayal of myself, but I had a renewed purpose that sustained me, and that was to someday be free and prove my innocence.

I was no longer living in the padded cell, but instead I was living in the general population wing.

I shared a room with another kid—a boy who had tried to murder his mother with a kitchen knife. We had a common area where the kids of the institution could watch TV shows and movies like *Star Trek: The Next Generation* and *Short Circuit*, play games like Connect Four and Mastermind, and exchange books. I was an avid reader and one of my favorite books that I read in the mental institution was Stephen King's *Pet Sematary*.

Of course, we weren't allowed to read horror books like that because of what they might do to our minds, but someone had snuck a copy in. Something about reading the horrors of a make-believe world and the struggles to overcome their challenges and mistakes gave me comfort and conviction.

These books and movies and TV shows would eventually influence my own writing of short stories and SciFi thrillers as I would often write about heroes overcoming incredible odds as a means of a mental and spiritual escape. They gave me hope that I was going to make it out of there.

I was going to figure this out.

Some of my institution mates I spent time with were arsonists, cutters, schizophrenics, manic-depressives, sadists, suicidal, devil worshippers, bullies, and the bullied. At their core, when you took away the stigma of mental illness, they were *people*. They had dreams and aspirations matched up with imbalances and unsupportive circumstances. Some of them even grew to become my friends. Others, not so much.

I was small for my age and younger compared to the rest of the population, and some of them bullied and abused me— verbally and physically. Until one day when I'd had enough. I may have had to be there against my will, but there was no way that I was going to let someone push me around anymore.

After being on the receiving end of one shove too many, my temper flared, and I launched a fist into the bully's face. This became a common occurrence, and even though I didn't always win the fights, after a few incidents like that, they would think twice before coming after me. And I'll admit, it felt really good to embrace the darkness inside of me. If I pretended I set fires because I was angry, shouldn't I at least get some benefit out of it?

During the day, the angry kid with the dark side became my identity. I was walking around tough to fool the inmates, making up stories to fool the doctors, and making progress toward getting out of this hell.

But then at night, under the covers, I would cry myself to sleep, wondering, *Who am I? Which me is the real me? Where does the lie stop and the truth begin?*

I didn't know anymore.

***

What I did know was that I would get very excited when my family came to visit. Even in my angry state, I knew they didn't send me to the mental institution to punish me; they had sent me here because they thought I needed help. In a terrible twist of fate, they had accidentally sent the wrong kid.

And since I was one of 6 kids at the time, I didn't really know who set the fires.

So when my family came to visit, I would just try to enjoy the day. I would draw for my mom and dad. Mostly dinosaurs that I had learned about: tyrannosaurus rex, ankylosaurus, dimetrodon, and more. I would play with my brothers on the jungle gym and play catch with the football on the field in the surrounding grounds, all the while knowing that one of them had committed the crime I was locked up for, and *he* would be allowed to leave.

And when they left, my heart was broken, but I was inspired and renewed to find a way out.

Eventually, I was deemed ready to return home.

It was one of the happiest moments of my life when my father came to pick me up to take me home. After 3 long years, I was finally getting out of this prison of the mind, body, and spirit.

The first weeks home were exciting and exhilarating—but they also filled me with dread at the same time. I was waiting for another fire to start. Waiting for the nightmare to repeat itself all over again. How long would I be locked away for next time? I stayed up late, watching to see which of my brothers would get up. But after a month or so, I settled in. And after a year, I began to relax. I was home.

Every day, however, I had to live a lie. I was still that kid who tried to burn down his house. No matter how well I did in school, or in sports, or in clubs, I still felt a darkness inside me: the negative side effects of wearing a dark mask of deception and living a lie for so long.

At 13, I turned to writing one of my first short stories (the one I would find under the stairs later in life), *Chronicles of the Warrior Lost*. A story about a child who was born into a super soldier experiment and trained to kill:

I was genetically altered while still in the womb. I am designed to be a type of super soldier. From birth my brain was fed only what they wanted me to hear. I was going to be loyal and faithful and question not what I was commanded to do.

They didn't count on me having superior intelligence, they just heightened my senses and increased my potential for performance and tolerance to pain. By age 10 I pretty much had a handle on how things worked and what was going on with the experiment though I didn't let on that I knew.

I created a character that was young and suffering just like me, but he was able to find a way to escape from the darkness by turning on his captors and using his powers for good. This gave me hope and allowed me to hold on for better days to come. Sometimes holding on is the best we can do.

NOW

The truth eventually came out, which marked the beginning of a whole new journey of struggle and self-discovery for me and my family as we'll see in the section on forgiveness, but for now, I want to hone in on the number one thing that helped me get through this ordeal.

I didn't fully realize it as I was going through the suffering, but it was the power of love. Even when I was utterly alone, I still knew there was love, care, and compassion in the world, and I felt it in my heart. Despite having my freedom and identity taken from me, I still had a life to live and an inner drive to survive

Before the mental institution, my mom and dad had shown me how much they loved me. My dad, in an ironic twist, was a volunteer firefighter. I remember when he brought a big, bright red firetruck to my elementary school for an epic show-and-tell. I remember how my mom would take care of all of us kids, cook for us, and ensure homework was done and we were in bed on time while my dad was working overtime. So even when I was locked away, I knew they had not stopped loving me.

Even though there were a lot of things messed up about the living conditions in the mental institution, there were a couple of nurses that showed they really cared about helping people.

I realized that many people labeled mentally ill by society—and facing the ramifications of the stigma that come along with that label—were actually good people at heart.

I also realized that even though I had to lie about who I was, I was developing enough self-worth to stand up for myself and believe a better day was coming, even if I didn't know when that day would arrive. Hoping and believing and having the faint, distant hint of love surrounding it all is how I got through it.

Granted, there are situations where people don't have these conditions. They cannot see the better day around the corner. They do not know that they matter. Or they don't have parents or family who love them or believe in them.

Let me tell you this, even if I've never met you: I believe in you and your ability to figure things out. Daniele believes in you. We both love you.

How can we say that?

Because we *practice* unconditional love and because we are all human and we share a common bond of connection as an extended family of brother and sisters.

You and I have the same body parts, our bodies are made up of the same types of cells, and we have 99.9% similarity in our DNA. We all have what you could call a soul, spirit, or simply a spark of life. We are far more alike than we are different.

Our unconditional love is a celebration of that which we have in common. We are unique as individuals, but we are united in the fact that all of humanity has faced struggle, and we have moved forward. Just as you are moving forward right now simply by reading this book, and we honor you and love you for that.

I hope you can feel it and know it in your heart as you read these words.

The 3 Love Lessons that follow will provide more knowledge and some of the best tactics, tools, techniques, and daily *practices* to bring more love into your life for you, your loved ones, and everyone you interact with.

But before we do that, let's check in with Daniele and learn how being diagnosed with a chronic disease and losing a parent as a child shaped her into the bold, loving leader of leaders she is today.

DANIELE'S STORY: LOVE

"Darkness cannot drive out darkness; only light can do that. Hate cannot drive out hate; only love can do that."
—Martin Luther King, Jr.

Death is the color of black on a starless, moonless, stormy night.
It tastes like eating your own flesh and blood.
And it sounds like a shrill scream piercing the night air.
Death smells like rotting corpses in a morgue.
It looks like family and friends crying at your loved one's funeral.
And it makes me feel all alone in a dark, desolate, isolated world.
—Daniele Shapiro, Grade 7

That poem was my first piece of published writing, featured in *A Celebration of Pennsylvania's Young Poets, 1995 edition.* I was thirteen years old and had just experienced the sudden and life-altering death of my father less than one year prior.

Combined with the never-ending need to take care of my diabetes so that I could simply remain alive each day and night, the death of my father the day after my twelfth birthday pushed me over an edge within my mental state that, until then, I had not known existed.

I became "clinically" depressed, according to mental health professionals. I constantly wondered what I did to deserve both a lifetime of incurable disease and to never be able to see or speak with my own father again. I blamed myself for both of these circumstances; both of which were completely out of my control, and there was nothing I could do to change either of them. It was an excruciatingly painful state to live in. That self-blame led to self-loathing, and I had no idea love was the answer to all of this.

There was nothing I or my parents could have done to prevent me from getting diabetes. There was nothing I could have done to stop my father from dying. I know this now, and I say it for a very important reason.

I am willing to bet that right this very second, you are blaming yourself for something that is completely out of your control, and that includes any and all past experiences. Obviously we can't change the past, and living there mentally and emotionally causes immense stress, fear, and pain that often manifests physically. You are probably asking yourself the same questions I was asking myself, presupposing that you are to blame and are unlovable, unforgivable, unwilling to love and forgive others, inferior, unworthy, incomplete, or broken.

Because it is likely that, just as I used to feel for so many years, you don't feel that you deserve love. Maybe you feel you aren't worthy of giving love, receiving love, or feeling loved—or that you are not enough for this world in one or many aspects of your life. Maybe you've even convinced yourself that you don't want to experience love at all.

It is my sincere hope that you come to realize the truth as I did—that you are loving and lovable, forgiving and forgivable, you are enough now, always have been, and always will be.

I am a different person now. I am no longer wishing my life was different, wondering if I would or could ever feel happy. Finally, and consciously, I chose to embrace the inevitability of change. I recognized that my (in the past, unconsciously conditioned, and now, consciously reconditioned) beliefs and choices were the only things I could control in this world, and further, that my beliefs and choices, the things I actually had control over, also shaped my day-to-day emotional experiences and feelings—my entire experience of life and how I interacted with others.

My beliefs and choices are the vehicles that carried me to the other side of hate and darkness, to the always open arms of love and light, toward myself and the Universe.

But I did not always know this crucial information regarding self-love and self-worth, as a concept and as a *practice*. Most people never do. Many adults remain that angst-filled teen or abused, neglected, abandoned child throughout their entire lives because the *practices* of self-love, self-care, intuition, healing, and mindfulness are sadly not subjects taught in traditional schooling.

These are the lessons people are left to figure out on their own and yet are the most critical to living a life filled with much more joy than pain—critical to understanding how to cope with the inevitable challenges of life in a healthy way, and how to bounce back from those challenges more quickly.

Becoming a master of these skills allows you to call gratitude, joy, and love your home-base emotions—your default emotions—the ones you automatically gravitate toward and feel more often than any others, instead of living in the unconsciously conditioned default emotions of fear, pain, anger, shame, guilt, and anxiety.

I am here to ask you to stop lying to yourself. Stop dimming your light. Stop believing that other people deserve better than you do. You may be experiencing circumstances that are difficult, but even in the darkest of days, nobody can dim your light but you. Only you can do it, and only you can stop doing it.

"No one can make you feel inferior without your consent." —Eleanor Roosevelt

ACT AS IF

You can choose to take one step forward—one step up. You can *act as if* you are the luminous, loving being you were born into this world to be, even if you don't believe it yet. Act as if you are just as deserving of experiencing the non-judgmental embrace and acceptance of love as anyone or anything else you can think of in the history of the world. Because you are. And I am, too. That is what I *know* to be true, without a shadow of a doubt.

Do this as often as you are willing. When I say act as if, I simply mean to *practice* being the way you desire to be in your life, even if you don't truly feel you are there yet. There is no perfect, only *practice*.

Your priorities dictate your *practices*, and your perspectives dictate your priorities, so it serves you to *act as if*—to *practice* being whom you know you want to be as often as possible. Eventually your perspectives will change, followed by your priorities, and there will be plenty of ebbs and flows along the way to be sure.

Love is the most powerful, free, readily available, infinitely renewable resource that exists on Earth and the one that can change your life more drastically than any other resource if you allow it to. Every human being has more love in them than they know what to do with, no matter their past or current circumstances or experiences.

I did not love myself, value myself, or believe I deserved to feel happy, healthy, vibrant, energetic, or joyful. Once I realized that, I began to finally understand that regardless of disease or any other circumstance, all humans can choose to walk a path of healing, and my life was never the same again. I chose to begin healing my spirit with love and to admit my overall worthiness of all good things, which in turn began healing my mind and body as well. I chose to break the patterns of my learned nature of fear and recondition my true nature of love.

I chose to un-condition fear and re-condition love, and it was the best choice I've ever made.

Love, specifically self-love, was the only thing that could save me, and it is the only thing that can save you, no matter what you're seeking salvation from. I am so grateful that I was, after years of internal turmoil, eventually willing to become vulnerable and let go of—*surrender*—all of my preconceived notions, judgments, and ideas about love, spirituality, personal growth, and other concepts that aren't always easily logically explained or measured. This change finally led me to understand and embrace my ability to control the one and only thing in this life that I truly could control: my choices. The same goes for you.

With that in mind, I consciously and intentionally choose love. Before everything I do, I say to myself, "I choose love." Before joining a conversation. Before writing an email. Before answering a question, whether asked by another or asked of myself. Before writing a blog. Before filming a video. Before making a decision. Before doing or saying anything to anyone.

Before considering the validity of any random thought that pops into my mind. In moments of indecision and disagreement. Day in and day out. Over and over again.

I've chosen to hang a piece of art directly over the foot of my bed so that love is the first thing I see when I wake and the last thing I see before going to sleep—it is the *LOVE* sculpture that sits in Love Park in my hometown of Philadelphia.

Minute by minute, second by second, I choose love. Now, love is my most deeply ingrained and best habit. Now, *I am love.* What will you choose?

YOUR STORY PART 3: LOVE

"Compassion for others begins with kindness to ourselves."
—Pema Chödrön

What lessons have you learned? What thoughts on your own story, on your Next Level Life have started coming up?

One of the goals we kept in mind while writing our stories on love was expanding our definition of love from a feeling we have for something or someone, to a powerful energy source that permeates all creation. An energy source that is in and around all of existence as we know it.

It's the love of progress, innovation, and solving the challenges of humanity on a global scale that keep entrepreneurs like Steve Jobs, Elon Musk, and Peter Diamandis fired up and focused on trying—no matter what failures might arise.

It's the love of the craft and following their passions for storytelling that keeps writers like Stephen King, James Patterson, and J. K. Rowling bringing to life amazing, terrifying, and magical worlds.

And it's the love of competition, sports, and pushing themselves to new heights that athletes like Michael Phelps, LeBron James, and Serena Williams demonstrate.

You don't have to be a celebrity-status successful person to experience these same feelings toward life, though they serve as a good example of how love can be more than just a vague concept you focus heavily on once a year on Valentine's Day.

Who do you love? Who loves you? What do you love to do? What do you love about yourself? What do you love about the Earth? Please don't filter or judge yourself in any way on these questions!

How can you make love a (much) bigger part of your Next Level Life Story?

These next three lessons will help guide you on your path to answer these questions.

LOVE LESSONS INTRO

"Let us always meet each other with a smile, for the smile is the beginning of love."
—Mother Teresa

Welcome to the Love Lessons. To start off, let's talk about what love is, and as you proceed, we encourage you to do so with an open mind and an open heart, actively dismissing old judgements that are bound to pop up.

Love encompasses a wide variety of emotions and states of mind. Many emotions and actions fall under the umbrella of love such as kindness, empathy, generosity, gratitude, acceptance, and more. Love is a feeling—an energy force that permeates our actions. It is a power source that can drive you to do things you never thought you'd be able to do.

We see this in the unconditional love of a parent for a child, or how the love of a person for their partner can drive them to do things they wouldn't do for themselves. Love is a cause, but it is also an effect. Love is a powerful tool that is available to you *at all times*; however, not everybody knows what love is or how many beneficial ways we can use it to serve our wellness and that of others.

Not everyone is taught what love is in a direct way. Not everyone has loving parents to provide a clear example of true love in action. Sometimes, people's example of love is something they see on TV or in a movie or read in a book. We're all basically coming up with our own definitions—our own realities of what love is, what it means, and how we define it. Believe it or not, these meanings and definitions can vary wildly from person to person.

Because love can mean so many things, what we're going to do for these three lessons is make it easy to win—make it easy to love. We will do that by broadening the ways we can *practice* love and accumulating small, meaningful wins because if you're reading this, chances are this might be an area of challenge for you as it was for me and as it is for so many people for so many reasons.

Another form of love that is useful to consider as you move forward is agape (pronounced: ah-GAH-pee). This is an active, powerful, unconditional love. A soul level love if you will. Taken in that context, this passage from the New Testament is an excellent way to consider and *practice* love:

Love is patient, love is kind. It does not envy, it does not boast, it is not proud. It does not dishonor others, it is not self-seeking, it is not easily angered, it keeps no record of wrongs. Love does not delight in evil but rejoices with the truth. It always protects, always trusts, always hopes, always perseveres. Love never fails. —1 Corinthians 13:4-8

If loving yourself and others is not a challenge for you, if you've got this area whipped, this section will help you level-up your love game and show others how to love even more throughout their lives.

LOVE LESSON 1: FOR YOURSELF

"You yourself, as much as anybody in the entire universe, deserve your love and affection."
—Buddha

BY DANIELE

The first part of walking the path of self-love is learning and implementing the tools and *practices* that cultivate, nurture, and grow the act of self-love into a default habit for the rest of your life. Gratitude is a mandatory, unignorable tool and *practice* that ultimately leads to understanding and fully embracing self-love.

Practicing gratitude is practicing self-love.

The most important thing to embrace first and foremost is that love is both a noun and a verb, and so is gratitude (I realize that grammatically speaking, gratitude is not a verb; however, for this particular purpose, I'm speaking figuratively about how gratitude must be put into action for it to be transformative).

The easiest way to express love is via expressing gratitude, and only when we put gratitude into action will we begin to see the immense power it holds. It is one of the few tools we have available to us at *every single moment in our lives* that produces immediate results when used with intention.

Gratitude breaks negative patterns in the moment. If you choose to use gratitude as a tool in your mind, body, spirit tool belt to keep you on track—and when you veer off, to course-correct toward what you do want—it is one that will serve you forever. In my opinion, it is the most powerful tool we have to alter our mental, physical, and spiritual states at any time.

Prioritizing the *practice* of daily self-love and gratitude expression allows you to open the previously locked or even undetected door to self-love. Then it is up to you to walk through—over and over and over again. Once you consciously and intentionally shift your focus from the default thoughts of scarcity and fear—what you do not have or do not want—to abundance and gratitude for the massive blessings that fill your life every day, self-love is inevitable.

Practicing self-love is like watering a neglected plant that, in order to thrive, needs to be watered daily. Eventually, it will regain its vitality, and before you know it, it will surpass its original circumstances and create new buds, flowers, leaves, and oxygen that without daily water would have been absolutely hopeless. You are that plant, and self-love is that water.

Learning how to access self-love as part of your being is crucial to feeling fulfilled in all areas of your life, because self-love, or the lack thereof, dictates the dynamic of every single relationship you ever have. This is true of the relationship you have with yourself, as well as all external relationships with everyone in the world, whether you realize it or not.

If you do not love yourself or you believe you are unlovable or unworthy of love—that negative, rejecting energy will spill outward, and others will unconsciously react to it, which you will observe in the way others treat you. People will generally treat you with the level of respect you treat yourself with, so if you are noticing a pattern in your life of people treating you poorly, I would be willing to bet that the most important person in your life—you—is also treating you poorly.

I challenge you to put this to the test. Is there an area of your life you feel massively confident about? How do you interact with and speak to yourself and others when involved in that area? What sort of language do you use? What thoughts do you have? Conversely, is there an area of your life where you feel you are lacking or not "good enough"? Now think about your interactions with yourself and others in the context of that situation, including the thoughts you have and the language you use.

THE HABIT OF SELF-LOVE

When self-love is a habitual part of your being, when love is who you are at your core, no matter the external circumstances or whether or not you feel confident about a situation, your self-love will give you the attitude and energy to know that even if you do not know the answer *now*, you believe in your ability to figure things out.

If you are of the belief that you are not deserving of love (your own or otherwise), yet you believe any other human being is deserving of love in any capacity, please always keep this in mind: throughout the lives of all humans that ever existed, every single one of us has done things we deeply regret. We have all hurt ourselves and other people, whether intentionally or not. We have all made decisions that, even in the moment we were making them, we knew they were wrong and we went ahead and did it anyway.

You are not the only person who has made terrible decisions, and your terrible decisions aren't somehow worse or less forgivable than anyone else's. That's it. End of story. If you believe that anyone else in the world is deserving of love but you aren't, please take some time to examine the extreme fault with the story you are making up to justify this excuse that has no base in reality.

Stop pretending that your "badness" or "sins" or whatever you want to call them are unforgivable, or that you are the only one who has committed acts they are embarrassed or ashamed of. We've all done it. We all still do it to some extent and likely always will. We're all human. Let it go. Allow yourself to move forward.

If you are used to looking for validation from external relationships, this is where self-love created and sustained by consistent *practices* will begin to completely shift your consciousness into a knowing that you are, always have been, and always will be the only validation you need when you think and act from a place of love. When that does finally happen, the way you interact with others will automatically begin to change to reflect your new *practices* regarding how you treat yourself and how genuinely and fully you appreciate what you have. It will truly feel like magic.

NOW IS ALWAYS THE BEST TIME FOR GRATITUDE

Gratitude for what you have *right now* and the willingness to prioritize time to care for yourself each day anchors self-love to your soul. It reminds you of your infinite worth and everything you can do, which strengthens and fortifies your appreciation for yourself, your life, and all the people you have met and experiences you have had throughout your life—good, bad, or otherwise.

Then you can choose to put gratitude into overdrive, to take it a step further. You will reach a whole new level when you choose to express gratitude for all the experiences you have ever had—whether you have deemed them negative or positive—accepting that all of them have shaped your character, your values, and your moral compass in life thus far.

If you have allowed any of these people or experiences to shape your character into something you are not currently happy with, you can use gratitude to reshape those character traits into the ones you consciously desire. As Maya Watson said, "learning is a gift, even when pain is your teacher." We must express gratitude for all gifts of learning, even the painful ones.

Full disclosure, having the ability to express gratitude or love for—or even look back on and bless—situations that you may currently categorize as horrible, scarring, terrifying, disgusting, immensely painful, gut-wrenching, or any other extremely negative descriptor, is not easy. However, when you do choose to take that gigantic step toward healing and clearing out the old to make room for the new, your life will never be the same again.

There are many ways to *practice* self-love—through all manner of self-care and gratitude, from writing things you are grateful for about yourself and why you are grateful for them daily (journaling of any kind, really), to gratitude stacking (one of my favorite *practices*, which I'll share with you in the Take Action section), to meditating, to walking outside in nature, standing barefoot on the grass, sand, or dirt, to practicing yoga, to implementing visual reminders such as vision boards, posters, or art that remind you to be grateful, to sharing your story vulnerably with the world in service to others and the oneness of all things that exist, and so many more.

For me, the ultimate expression of self-love is to give of yourself to others—to serve. This service cannot be done in full authenticity until you've accepted that self-love is key in every single interaction you ever have. This is accomplished first and foremost via service in kindness, love, acceptance, empathy, and tolerance, and service in the knowing—that is reflected in your actions—that everyone and everything you come in contact with is your family—your Earth family. We are all part of the same human family. We are one. We all deserve love and forgiveness.

Everything changes for the better—*life feels better*—when you express gratitude for the Universe and *all* people and things that inhabit it, including yourself. This will likely require a shift in your perspective. For some, it will require an extreme shift from feeling like you are a random and unimportant part of some chaotic existence, to feeling like your actions—your existence—are deeply in service to the greater good of all existence. The more self-love you *practice*, the more intense your intuitive *knowing* that your role in this Universe is powerfully meaningful becomes.

Living in a state of self-love—a simple yet profound love of all that you are *just because you exist and needing no other reason at all*—allows unlimited room for growth into the acceptance of the oneness of everything. Not just on this planet, but in the entirety of the Universe. Becoming conscious of the role we play, the energy we create, the role of having complete and total ability to either choose to express or ignore self-love in any given moment, allows us to live in love literally all the time, even (and especially) in challenging times that are inevitable parts of life for everyone.

The secret to living a fulfilled life is giving, particularly giving self-love *unconditionally* to yourself. This allows you to genuinely be of service to others and expect nothing in return other than the fulfillment you feel internally for acting in alignment with your true energy—the energy of love. Giving that love freely is a powerful act of self-love for all that you were, are, and ever will be.

TAKE ACTION

This book will be of even greater benefit to you when you take action along with reading the words. Reading and contemplating are great tools, but when you take actions such as journaling and performing the *practices* we suggest, you'll make faster progress in ways you can't even imagine. Taking physical action along with the mental side of reading locks in the lessons and creates anchors that lead you back to your desired outcome much more habitually.

Gratitude Stacking (Specific to the *Practice* of Self-Love):
I do this every single day, sometimes multiple times per day. It is the most powerful and immediately effective exercise that you can choose to *practice* in order to create an immediately healing state of gratitude anytime, anywhere. This *practice* instantly changes your mental, physical, and spiritual state, no matter what is going on around you—no matter where you are or what emotions you are feeling.

There is no location or circumstance that can prevent you from practicing gratitude stacking. Here's how to do it:

If possible, find a place that is quiet, although silence and solitude are not requirements. You can do this anywhere. One of my clients told me she goes into the bathroom at her job, shuts the door, and does this in the bathroom stall. You can do this at home, at the gym, or on public transportation. You can literally do this anywhere you choose, anytime.

Close your eyes, put your hand over your heart, *feel it beating*, and begin concentrating on your breathing, making sure to begin taking deep, full breaths, feeling your stomach rise and fall with each breath. (If you cannot sit down, close your eyes and place your hand over your heart for some reason; you can absolutely do this standing up, with your eyes open, and with your hands anywhere you want. I just happen to prefer the sitting or lying down, eyes closed, hand over heart setup whenever possible—it's a form of meditation for me.)

Your breathing is your top focus. Breathe in and breathe out, feeling your stomach rise with each inhalation. While doing this, think of all the things about yourself that you are grateful for (if you want to focus more on outward things, you can also add in things, people, experiences, achievements, and circumstances you are grateful for outside of yourself, but I recommend focusing mostly on self-love until you know that is part of you on a cellular level, then expand outward from there)—literally everything you can possibly think of that you are grateful for now or have ever been grateful for about yourself in your entire life.

Begin listing—saying them out loud or silently—every single thing you are grateful for and why:

- I am grateful for my lungs because they allow me to breathe the oxygen that sustains me.
- I am grateful for my smile because it allows me to communicate love in any language.
- I am grateful for my heart because it beats more than one hundred thousand times each day, keeping me alive without me having to ask.
- I'm grateful for my body—my perfectly imperfect body that is always there for me and has gotten me through 100% of my life so far.
- I am grateful for my skin because it lets me feel and interact with the incredible world around me.
- I'm grateful to be alive so I can share my true nature of love and light with others.

If you think you don't have anything to be grateful for, it means your old, default stories, meanings, and mindset habits are trying to pull you back to fear and negativity and away from love and gratitude. This is a good time to think of all the things you may unconsciously take for granted—the things that, if they disappeared, your entire life would be noticeably, and in some cases massively, less enjoyable.

If you are here reading this book, you could say "I'm grateful that someone loved me enough to teach me how to read, so I can literally learn anything I want anytime I want." If you have food to eat, you could say "I'm grateful for the food I have to eat and to the Earth for providing the ingredients because they help me sustain my health." "I'm grateful and blessed to have clean water and I acknowledge that a large portion of the world does not have access to it."

Express gratitude for having clothing and shoes to wear—and likely a wide variety of them. If you need medication and have access to it, express gratitude for that, as I can say from personal experience that a giant source of gratitude for me is having access to the medication I require multiple times a day, every day. If you have a relationship with anybody in your life who brings you joy and lifts you up, express gratitude for them. Express gratitude for all the lessons that pain has taught you. Express gratitude for your family, friends, and pets. Express gratitude for any and every little or big thing that has ever taught you a lesson that opened up room for you to grow.

Or, you can just say "thank you." As the thirteenth-century theologian and philosopher Meister Eckhart so perfectly stated, "If the only prayer you ever say in your entire life is thank you, it will be enough."

I recommend doing this exercise for, quite literally, *any* amount of time. From thirty seconds to infinity. I have practiced this mindset for so long that I go to bed in this state and wake up in it—on purpose. For those of us who are on a schedule, gratitude stacking for thirty seconds to five minutes daily will always have an incredibly profound and immediate effect on your state of mind.

Today's action item is to choose a specific amount of time (any amount of time will make a big difference!), schedule it in your calendar, and *practice* gratitude stacking. I can only hope that you choose to go back and use this tool all the time, especially when you notice you are in a negative thought pattern of any sort. Just like any tool, gratitude stacking is only effective when we use it. Gratitude is the *best* way to break any negative pattern.

LOVE LESSON 2: FOR OTHERS

"Whenever we manage to love without expectations, calculations, negotiations, we are indeed in heaven."
—Rumi

BY BILL

Often times, when I tell the story of my time in the mental institution, people say something along the lines of, "I can't imagine what kind of love you tapped into to forgive your brother and parents and come together to heal."

To that, my reply is, "It wasn't easy... But it was worth it!"

Although forgiving and choosing to love my family was a decision I made consciously and altruistically to move toward the greater good in the situation, it was also the best choice for me as an individual. I could let the circumstances get me down and make me bitter, or I could seek a way to make myself and my family stronger. When I framed it that way, the choice was clear. I chose love.

That all sounds well and good, but *choosing* to love... How do you do it? How do you love others more? And why?

Maybe you've been through a difficult situation in your life—or are going through one right now—that tore you up inside and made you angry or depressed. How can you rise above this situation? How can you empower yourself to love more in your life? That is what this lesson is all about. While it is paramount to love yourself first, you can enhance that power by giving your love freely to others and without expectation of reciprocity.

GIVE THE GIFT OF LOVE, AND EVERYONE BENEFITS

One of the greatest joys of living is giving to others—giving our time, our presence, and our unique gifts and talents. When we think of love as a gift or simply an act of kindness, then we can start to find ways to increase our love output.

The key to loving others is to become aware of all the ways you can do it so you can seek out opportunities to *practice* it more often and more easily. Why? Because the more loving we are to others, the better we feel about ourselves and the more we open ourselves up to the good feelings in life.

You can start with your family, whether as a parent, a child, a sibling, a cousin, a guardian, or any of the myriad of familial relationships we have in life. Then we look to expand beyond that to friends, classmates, coworkers, our community, and beyond. The goal is to extend this *practice* beyond your comfort zone, to people who are seemingly total strangers (though "stranger" is a matter of perspective—there are so many ways we are all connected). That is when you will really start to have a more fulfilling life.

Look for code words for love. Some of love's code words are:

- Passion
- Compassion
- Kindness
- Gratitude
- Appreciation
- Forgiveness
- Empathy

You can access these code words through your actions. They can be in the form of a smile, a kind word, a kiss, a hug, a handshake, saying "thank you" or "you're welcome," saying "I forgive you," "I'm sorry," or simply pursuing what you are passionate about through creating, learning, and taking action on your goals and dreams.

Expressing kindness equals expressing love. Treating others as you would like to be treated is often the golden rule, but sometimes it isn't. I say you should treat others better than you would like to be treated, because I can be pretty harsh on myself, even when I know that doesn't always serve me best (and am reminded of this often by Daniele!) I find it useful to make it a *practice* to treat others better than I would treat myself, and doing so acts as a reminder to treat myself with that same love and kindness.

HOLD THE DOOR

An act of kindness could be something as simple as holding the door for somebody. It could be as simple as seeing a friend who is down and asking them how their day is going and if there is anything you can do to help them smile. Be their shoulder to lean on or offer a sympathetic ear.

This habit will expand and grow over time. Like a muscle, it grows stronger with *practice*. It won't just be friends you choose to help, and you won't just be holding doors—likely you'll soon be volunteering your time to serve the greater good. Perhaps you'd enjoy helping at an animal shelter, at a local hospital, or doing meal preparation for a local non-profit that feeds those in need. The options to help others are endless.

One of the master keys to loving others is to ensure that it is a *selfless* and *unconditional* love. What does that mean? That means you *practice* giving love without any expectation of reciprocation. This ensures that you receive the benefit of being a loving person without having to depend on others to return that love (which could really save you from a lot of pain).

Many people find themselves looking to others to "complete them," and they look for that external validation as a feeling of love to fuel them rather than realizing that they are already whole and complete. They give love with the strong expectation and even demand of love in return, and if and when that love is not returned, that can create a sense of loss, suffering, and unworthiness that are entirely misplaced and can never be satisfied externally as that feeling of unconditional love being sought can only be filled from within.

This doesn't mean that you can't bask in the warm glow of someone's love—of the energetic exchange of mutual love—it just means that you must be carefully conscious so that you do not become addicted to the feeling of someone else's love that leaves you feeling empty or incomplete when you are alone. We can *practice* doing that and get stronger and stronger in that regard by giving love unconditionally as often as possible, including to yourself.

Take for instance Daniele and myself. We love each other very much—so much so that sometimes it is overwhelming to even consider that we have the capacity to love another person to the extent that we do. And even though we give each other our space, we do spend a lot of time together—hanging out, working together, traveling together, writing together, giving talks together, and so much more. It works out so well with us because we've done the work to get us to this point, and trust us, it took a lot of work!

At our cores, we *practice* unconditional love and self-love, and are fiercely independent people in general. So our coming together is a selfless collaboration that creates its own entity—the hive-mind as we sometimes call it—but we're still whole and complete as individuals.

Let me give you an example using the simple suggestion of holding the door for others. I was raised by my father to say "thank you" when someone does something for you, as a matter of good manners and respect. Pretty good rules to live by in my opinion. But later in life, I found myself running into the classic dilemma of expectation of reciprocation. When I would hold the door for someone at a convenience store, for instance, and they didn't say thank you, I would get mad. I would say aloud, sarcastically, "You're welcome!"

Yikes! Kind of douchey of me, I know. But maybe you've had a similar experience before?

The problem was that I was basing my sense of joy for performing an act of kindness on the other person's choice to acknowledge and appreciate my action. However, when you flip the script—when the burst of joy you feel is about the *act* of holding the door for them, no matter the response—you are already winning. And if they do say thank you? Then let that enhance your feeling further. But ensure that you're not seeking it. It sets you up for a win-win situation.

Look for areas in your life where you can perform these acts of kindness, and you will feel the love increase. When you combine this idea of loving others with self-love, the world takes on a new, more fulfilling experience.

BE LIKE A LOVE SUN

Another tool I use is to imagine your essence, your spirit, your spark of life emanating like a "Love Sun" from your core. This Love Sun shines our love brightly wherever we go.

The more ways you find to be loving to yourself and others, the better you feel—and the better the people around you feel. In our solar system the sun shines its light unconditionally and life abounds on our planet because of it. Seeing that visualization helps me embody that selflessness in my acts of kindness and unconditional love *practices*, and I encourage you to try it out for yourself.

Here's where I take a time out for my masculine-minded readers who just read that and are about to throw this book away and are saying, "A Love Sun? Really?"

Yes, really.

Masculinity, and being "a man" in many ways comes down to how much love you can share, how you care for and protect your loved ones and do what's right and just in the world because you have a love for life that's so powerful that its light can't be diminished. Shine on Love Sun. Shine on.

"I think a man's masculinity is tested by how much LOVE he is able to spread. When spreading love, he becomes the protector of emotions, softness, while being present with everyone—that's what it means to be a real man." –Wim Hof

TAKE ACTION

Grab your journal and list three people you love, three people you want to be kind to, and then at least once a day, say to yourself, "I'm going to perform an extra act of kindness for them." Recognize, acknowledge, and celebrate the act within yourself, even if the person you performed the act of kindness for doesn't recognize it. Allow yourself to purposely feel good for having performed that action.

Hold the door. Practice holding the door and allow yourself to feel that burst of love, selflessly. Bonus points if you get the *Game of Thrones* reference!

LOVE LESSON 3: FOR THE WORLD

"We are all connected—to each other biologically, to the Earth chemically, to the rest of the Universe atomically."
—Neil deGrasse Tyson

Love is a path to a kinder, more caring world. We've come so far already in our lessons on our path of love, from learning and practicing how to love yourself more to giving love to strangers without expecting anything in return. We have learned that we are worthy, that we are all whole and complete just as we are, that it's okay for us to dream big and want to do more and be more with our life without internal judgement.

We've also learned the importance of showing compassion, kindness and love for others, whether verbally or through a gesture—small acts of kindness strengthen your love muscles. We've been expanding our circle of love and influence along the way.

Even if you've just been reading these lessons without taking, you are already starting to see the world in a different view. It's important for us to have a vision for a kinder, more caring world—a vision that takes us out of focusing solely on ourselves and embracing that we are all part of a much bigger whole.

We must be brave enough to create a vision that extends to the future and sees the world moving toward love, forgiveness, and progress, even and especially when things seem bleak. Seeing the world in that way can be a big challenge, but big challenges like that would do well to get you excited since we know about how all meaningful growth and progress comes out of meeting challenges with a we-will-figure-this-out attitude.

Big challenges inspire creativity and innovation. When people see the love you are demonstrating in the world, they see it as a sign, as a light they are drawn to—your light. You are giving them permission, subconsciously, to shine their love more as well.

There have been many challenging times when Daniele and I have been surrounded by love in our lives without recognizing it at the time. We can now look back and see how important that presence of love was for our development. It's important for us to remember to *be* that source of love for others. If they can see it and feel it, then they'll believe it. When people see you practicing love, they are subtly shifted inside themselves.

As you continue to develop your powers of love, your capacity to love and be loved, your compassion and acceptance even in times of disagreement—you will be a part of the movement toward a kinder, more caring world.

TAKE ACTION

Your action item is a creative thought experiment, so break out your journal, or set aside some time to meditate on it. Write this down or say it aloud: "What would happen to the world if everybody on this planet felt twice as much love for themselves and for others as they do now?"

Imagine if everybody from every country around the world felt twice the amount of love, performed twice the acts of kindness, twice the amount of selfless service. *What would that world look like? Feel like?*

What would happen to every child who was growing up, every grandparent who looked back on the lives of their families, every neighbor, community, and country across this planet? Please take a few minutes to really reflect on this in your journal.

Does it have to be realistic and based on the state of the world currently? No. It's a thought experiment that is only limited by your own willingness to imagine and feel. By looking at a world with grander possibility than we currently see, we start to find our place, our path, and our purpose just a little bit more clearly.

But we can say this with total certainty: what might not seem realistic now holds the potential to be very realistic in the future if enough people are willing to shift the way they think, feel, and act toward themselves and others. This shift starts with you.

Fifty years ago, the function of smart phones connected to the Internet with the ability to talk to anyone anywhere in the world at any time in seconds would seem like magic to many. Surely, we can make similar, seemingly magical shifts for the love of humanity in the next fifty.

"We" (as a collective human race) starts with "me" (as a single individual). As Gloria Steinem so clearly stated, "The future depends entirely on what each of us does every day."

HERO'S QUEST: LOVE

"Oh yes, the past can hurt. But, you can either run from it
or, learn from it."
—Rafiki

"You gotta put your behind in your past!"
—Pumbaa
The Lion King

The start of your adventure has been challenging, but your confidence grows with each step you take.

Especially since you have discovered your first reward: the Shield of Love!

On the front of the shield is the very same symbol that adorns this book, a heart with a brave soul ready to rise up and face the day head on. You hold the Shield of Love in your hand, and feel a gentle warmth emanating from it. It is light as a feather, for its power is channeled from your own inner light, and it is made stronger the more you discover and live into your purpose.

It protects you and is seen as a symbol of hope to everyone you encounter. It is a reminder that you are an energetic source of love and that you are always loved, even when there is no one other than yourself around to say the words.

With a renewed sense of purpose toward receiving this amazing treasure, you consult the magical tome and the mind map.

Next, it will take you through the treacherous path of the twisted forest where you must seek a magical, green artifact—the Orb of Forgiveness—which offers healing and focusing powers. You smile as you ready yourself to continue on your adventure.

Little do you know, the Orb of Forgiveness has a price that must be paid in order for you to possess it.

If it's a peaceful life that you want to live, you must master how to:

FORGIVE

BILL'S STORY: FORGIVE

THEN

When I was 14 years old, I was coming home from a trip with my family to the Adirondacks of Virginia. My parents would often pack all 6 of the kids in the station wagon (later an SUV) with a luggage shell on top and kids crammed in and travel all over the country. Sometimes it would be a straight shot drive overnight from New Jersey down Interstate 95 (I-95) all the way to Orlando and Disney World.

Another time it was a cross-country trip through Chicago, Mount Rushmore, Colorado, and the Hoover Dam, and then back through Texas on the way home. My parents weren't afraid to put some miles on the vehicle in order to have the experience of seeing the world.

This trip, however, was different.

We were stopped at a gas station and one of my brothers had gotten out of the car to run off. My father chased after him. I already had a very strong suspicion that the brother that ran off was the one who set the fire.

Even 3 years after being freed, I still thought of my time in the mental institution often. Everyone still believed I had set the fires, and now my goal was to figure out how to be free of the lies I was living.

Some moments have a momentous feeling to them, and this was one such moment. On a hunch, I gathered the courage and blurted out to my mom, "Maybe if he had the help I got in the mental institution, we wouldn't be in this situation!"

I expected my mom to yell at me, but her only reaction was to stare into my eyes. Her eyes were doubting and knowing all at once. I think she may have realized the truth of the matter in that very moment.

You see, as a child, I had always gotten good grades, always had a smile on my face, and was quick to try to brighten people's days with a joke or something silly. I generally steered clear of any trouble. My brother, on the other hand, was always getting in trouble at home and at school. It just didn't match up.

And in this moment, I could feel in the pit of my stomach that something big was about to go down.

My dad returned to the car with my brother, and my mom turned around in the front passenger seat and repeated what I had said.

And then the dam let loose.

My brother admitted it. "It was me," my brother said. "I did it."

My parents were in shock.

My brother was a wreck.

And I was smiling the biggest smile of my life for the whole ride home.

***

The drive home was a long, quiet one. My sister and the rest of my brothers could sense something major was going on, even if they had been too young at the time of the fires to remember the events very well.

The next day, my parents got together with me and told me how sorry they were. They were sincere and heartfelt, and I told them I forgave them. I honestly didn't even have to forgive them. I always knew they were doing what they thought was right for the right reason.

I didn't talk to my brother about it, and we drifted further apart than ever before. Eventually, he moved out of the house on his own.

As for me, I was focusing on how good it felt to be free! Free from the lies. Free from wearing the dark mask of deception.

But the good feelings didn't last long, because as the old saying goes, thoughts become things. I had pretended for so long that I was mentally disturbed, and even though I no longer had to live the lie, my thoughts were still dark.

And they scared me. This was supposed to be it, I thought. All should be well now!

But it wasn't.

How could I still be thinking these dark thoughts? Who was the person looking back at me from the mirror?

Again, I had a new goal in life. I was going to figure out how to rid myself of this darkness. I was determined to figure it out just like that 8-year-old boy Billy did.

I was still filled with so much anger. If a kid at school would make fun of me for any reason, I would punch him in the face, just like I did back in the mental institution.

I joined the wrestling team and got out some of my aggression on the mat, but it wasn't enough.

My dark thoughts and painful memories still haunted me. I would write about them in journals, school writing assignments, and short stories like this passage from *Chronicles of the Warrior Lost* where William led a rebellion and escaped from the complex:

"The scientists and guards were sworn to the cause of world domination. They destroyed the whole complex with preset charges so as to not leave a trail. Charge after charge went off. I kept moving to the entrance, debris falling on me, fire burning me. Almost to the top and all of the building imploded.

I awoke sometime later and luckily I was close to the top. I was able to escape. A young and broken human.

It's almost been 3 years since those incidents. I thought back about the program. All that I had learned. I made adjustments and improvements. I redesigned everything. My warrior program will excel me to what I once was and beyond."

I was writing about myself, years after escaping the mental institution, still trying to give myself a positive roadmap to move forward with my own life, being guided by the written word to find strength through adversity.

I've continued to write stories into adulthood featuring heroes persevering against massive challenges and overcoming incredible odds. In my Mars Journey series for instance, Brent Carlson, a brilliant but disgraced former astronaut, gathers and trains an international crew in order to get to Mars with plenty of cybernetically enhanced humans, rogue AI robots, and dark clandestine organizations to overcome along the way. Seems my story writing subject hasn't changed all that much since I was a kid!

Writing has the power to help us work through our own obstacles and help others at the same time. It's a powerful combination of entertainment and empowerment. In many ways, both writing and reading, whether it be fiction or non-fiction, prepares us to face the known and unknown alike.

During my senior year in high school, I was still searching for the solution to my dilemma. In Advanced Placement Science, I submitted a research paper on titled, *Correlations of Aggression in Athletes*. I was trying to find out why I was so angry. My experiment and research ended up being selected for the National Junior Science and Humanities Symposia finals. Despite my success in that arena, the true answers alluded me, and my thoughts got even darker.

After graduating, I moved 6 hours away from home to attend the University of Pittsburgh and quickly ran into a new complication: depression. I would stay holed up in my dorm room for days at a time. As an athlete in high school, I had chosen to never drink. In college, I decided to let loose.

The following 3 years were a battle back and forth between dropping out of college, sleeping on a friend's couch (avoiding homelessness by mere days), getting my own place above a bar, getting a job installing fences, partying heavily, going back to school and dropping out again, taking up martial arts, working toward something—anything.

In a moment of complete suffering, in a cell created of my own mind, I lashed out at the darkness in me. How could I let this monster inside me live? In my apartment after days of partying hard with friends, I smashed down the door to my room, punching it to wood splinters, and broke down sobbing on my bed. My friends comforted me, telling me it was going to be all right.

I wasn't so sure.

At my wit's end with tears streaming down my face, I shouted by way of pure stream of consciousness, "My brother never said he was sorry!"

Silence filled the room as the weight of my words sunk in to me.

I said it again with more clarity now.

"My brother never said he was sorry."

I had been holding on to all this anger, all this hurt and rage and despair for so many years because I held blame in my heart—because I harbored hostile feelings at the core of my being. Because negative energy had formed around my identity.

Shortly thereafter, I called my brother. We hadn't spoken in quite some time, and I told him what I had discovered.

"You never said you were sorry," I said.

And he replied, "Bill... I think of you every morning when I wake up and every night before I go to bed. I am filled with guilt and shame for what I did to you. And I am sorry. I am so sorry."

And I said, "I forgive you."

And in that moment when I forgave him, it was literally like a massive weight was lifted off my shoulders. I breathed the air in deeply. The world around me suddenly seemed a little bit brighter, and the darkness in me relinquished its power.

My brother and I continued our conversation. It turned out he had been going through a rough time in his own way, ever since he was a kid. By bearing the guilt for these acts, he was suffering just like I was, maybe even worse.

Later in life, we grew to become good friends. He's a good brother and a smart, kind human being who made mistakes when he was young like all humans do. And though it brought me so much peace to forgive him, it is one of my greatest hopes that he will one day forgive himself.

NOW

Forgiveness is a gift. It's a gift you give yourself and others, and it clears a path toward healing. We are going to discuss how you can add forgiveness in many of its forms to your tool belt. When you discover the power of forgiveness, when wielded in the right way in the right situation, you will wonder how you ever got along without it.

I would like to point out that just because I learned to forgive, it doesn't mean all my problems were miraculously solved overnight. It took many years and a never-give-up attitude to bring about lasting change (we'll discuss that in the perseverance section).

Many times when I tell this story, people get upset, which is understandable, but sometimes they get mad at my brother or my parents.

If you find yourself feeling that way right now, then this is the perfect time to *practice* forgiveness. Even if it's not something that was done to you directly, you may still harbor negative feelings. Or maybe there's something in your life that came to mind as you were reading this story. Maybe it's a good time to demonstrate forgiveness in that situation.

My situation was like a force of nature. Sometimes tornadoes hit us. Sometimes bad things happen. We can't change that. Hating the tornadoes gets you nowhere; it's how we respond in the moment and every moment moving forward into the future.

Two of my biggest heroes are my mom and dad, for raising all of us kids and persevering through an immensely challenging situation while instilling strong family values, a hard work ethic, and an amazing capacity for love. From our tragedy it is our heartfelt hope that you can find some lessons to apply to your life to make it feel better more often.

The following chapters will give you more tools, techniques, and tactics to bring forgiveness into your life on a daily basis. But first, let's check in with Daniele.

DANIELE'S STORY: FORGIVE

"Mistakes are always forgivable, if one has the courage to admit them."
—Bruce Lee

I used to believe I was broken and incomplete, not enough and not worthy of the good things in life. I didn't have the awareness yet to entertain the idea that I could choose a journey of healing (which for me simply means continually embracing my wholeness, my completeness, my unbrokenness) regardless of having an incurable disease, losing my father, or of any other circumstances.

The truth is I did have that power, as does everyone else in existence. I am whole. You are whole. Nothing is missing. Everything I need is and was always inside me, as it is in you. Embracing that reality is one of my definitions of healing.

Through the experience of my ongoing emotional, physical, and spiritual transformations—in addition to having the incredible blessing and privilege of figuratively walking side by side with thousands of others through their various transformations—I have learned that consciously choosing and engaging in the act of forgiveness can seem like the most difficult and elusive *practice* that exists.

I have also learned that if you believe something with even a small amount of conviction—and I mean anything—then it is true for you and for your mind, body, and spirit, regardless of whether anyone else believes it or if it is based in any semblance of logic or reason.

Anyone, no matter what, can choose a path of healing (accepting and embracing wholeness). The first step on that path must be forgiveness.

I used to believe that the ways I knowingly mistreated my whole self—mind, body, and spirit—were unforgivable, and as long as I continued to believe that, it was true for me. That "truth" echoed loudly in the emotions I felt every single day, as well as determining my dominant thoughts. This translated into how I interacted with the rest of the world, creating my very reality.

When I believed I was unforgivable, I automatically and unconsciously projected that belief onto everyone else. I rarely gave others the benefit of the doubt and defaulted to assuming the worst about other people based on how I felt about myself, often before I even had a conversation with them.

I consider love and forgiveness to be the most highly valuable and empowering gifts that we as human beings can choose to give to ourselves or others in any moment.

YOU ARE NOT UNFORGIVABLE

As I mentioned earlier, we have all done or continue to do things we regret, things that make us feel guilt, shame, pain, and more. We've all hurt ourselves and others. You are not unique in that way—simply human. Making terrible decisions (no matter how many or how often) is something that, if you are a human being, you cannot escape.

What you can escape is the mental trap and extremely mentally, physically, and spiritually stifling belief that you are unforgivable, especially if you believe any other humans are. We are all deserving of love and forgiveness, and there are no exceptions.

Through many extraordinarily difficult lessons learned while trying to make progress with my own health and happiness and continually running into the same walls, I finally figured out that the only way I could ever truly move forward with my life—with cultivating and nurturing the person I knew I wanted to be, that I knew was my truest self—was to love and forgive myself.

I knew I had to never give up on that decision no matter how many times I took steps backward, reverted to my old ways—regardless of how many times it felt like I failed, I eventually re-focused and got back on track. This took many years of failures, of iterating and re-iterating, years of willingness to change my original plan to fit the way my life was versus the way I thought it "should" be.

The only way I was able to start that process was to allow myself to become completely vulnerable—with myself. I had to surrender to the wildly unfamiliar but overwhelmingly freeing feeling of full and total acceptance of myself as a whole, complete being. The key was to accept myself as complete, unbroken, enough, worthy, and perfectly imperfect as I always was and always would be, just as all human beings are.

I finally understood that all the demons I was fearing and fighting every day were created by me. They were created by the stories I made up and the meanings I assigned to every circumstance I had ever experienced. After realizing that, examining that, and taking the time and self-care to replace my old stories with new meanings—all consciously and intentionally from a place of love and forgiveness—I truly understood what people meant when they say that happiness is a choice.

Accepting that you are whole *right now* and worthy of all good things in life starts with choosing to give yourself the gift of forgiveness.

Once you embrace the fact that you are the creator of your happiness in every moment based on how much love and forgiveness you are willing to *practice*, your life will never be the same. It will be a messy, uncomfortable, non-linear process that will include negative emotions, steps forward, and steps backward.

At the end of the day, only *you* can make you happy through living in your true nature of love—both towards yourself and others. We all have the same power as human beings to create that happiness by consistently *practicing* acknowledging all that you are, have, love, and feel any level of gratitude for, and forgiving yourself and others.

I am in no way indicating that it is not part of life to feel unhappy along the journey. In fact, it's quite the opposite. We must openly and nonjudgmentally allow ourselves to truly *feel* all our feelings so that we can work through them, acknowledge them—call them by their names and identify their sources so that we can better recognize them and how to heal through them (move back toward wholeness) when they inevitably continue to arise throughout our lives.

What I am saying is that choosing to constantly *live* in those negative feelings and focus your attention and thoughts on them consistently is another story entirely—a story only you can rewrite. A story who's rewriting begins with forgiveness.

Once you identify a recurring negative emotion and dig down to its source, which is often deeply rooted in the past, you can work through it in a variety of ways. There are many tools which we will cover in future chapters—but you won't be surprised to hear that they involve *practices* even and especially when you don't feel like doing them—conscious reconditioning. Un-conditioning fear and re-conditioning love.

NEGATIVE EMOTIONS ARE PART OF THE PROCESS

The goal isn't to avoid feeling negative emotions. The goal is to face those feelings and see them clearly so that they no longer control you and your experience of your life for elongated periods of time. The only way to get started on doing that is to forgive. Surrender yourself to the conscious and intentional act of forgiveness because you deserve it, and it works.

There was no one defining moment for me regarding forgiveness. I have accepted the fact that forgiveness, much like love and perseverance, are ongoing experiences and *practices* on this incredible journey of life. They are amazingly valuable and effective tools at our disposal to make life more joyful. But just like any tool, they are only helpful if we choose to use them over and over and over again.

I had to first forgive myself—completely and unconditionally. I forgave myself for the horrible things I said and did to my mind, body, and spirit. I forgave myself for the years of binge eating. I forgave myself for lying to my mom constantly and pushing her away when all she wanted to do was help and comfort me.

I forgave myself for the years of sedentary living and making up the story that I just wasn't "athletic." I forgave myself for the long period of time I spent not caring for or about my emotional and physical health. I forgave myself for the inappropriate blame I placed on myself for the death of my father and for having diabetes. I forgave myself for my nasty attitude toward so many people for so many years because I was in so much pain. I forgave myself for things I am not yet ready to share with the world.

Recently, while journaling, which is one of my daily self-love and self-care *practices*, I realized I had more forgiving to do. Through allowing my thoughts to come out on paper without judgment, structure, or rules of any kind, it came to light that I was angry at my father for dying more than twenty-three years prior.

Even with all the tools I have and use every day, I didn't realize I was burying that pain until I allowed my spirit, or my subconscious mind, to express itself without restriction or judgment on the pages of my journal. The biggest difference about this act of forgiveness versus any others I've had to work through is the quickness with which it transpired.

I talked to my mom and found out that she and my dad knew from a doctor's appointment that his heart was damaged from the years of smoking cigarettes and eating unhealthy food more than six months before he died of a heart attack. His doctor urged him to come in for preventative procedures in hopes of avoiding a heart attack, but he was scared, so he didn't.

My mom told me that my dad said that he knew that if he went into the hospital he was going to die there. I'll never have the chance to ask him why he accepted that belief, but I know that his acceptance of that story he made up was certainly a factor that contributed to his death.

This information made sense to me hearing it as an adult because I remember my dad taking me out to lunch at his favorite diner shortly before he died, the Dining Car. I believe he was doing his best to relay to me that he wasn't going to be around much longer. It didn't register to me back then as an eleven-year-old, but now thinking back on it, it clicked into place. He accepted his death before it happened.

I almost immediately forgave my father, both out loud and on the page. I finally understood fully that he was doing the best he could with the resources he had available, and I'm forever grateful for the many valuable lessons he taught me in life and in death, mostly by the way he showed love and kindness every day of his life.

Love, forgiveness, and perseverance are, like any skill or experience, easier to access and utilize the more you *practice*, much like a muscle that grows stronger with repeated workouts. You simply get better at using those tools, which makes a massive difference in your overall quality of life.

I also had to forgive diabetes. Forgiveness needs to be applied to all persons, places, things, experiences, and circumstances—animate or inanimate, visible or invisible, past or present. You see, the definition of forgiveness includes the cessation of negative feelings about or toward a person, place, thing, or experience, and diabetes feels like all of those at different times.

After a while, I truly ceased feeling any negative feelings toward diabetes, because diabetes is part of me, and I love me entirely. I used to always fight with my diabetes, but now I choose to embrace it. I love and accept it for what it is: a part of me. I treat it with love, forgiveness, and perseverance versus anger, fear, resentment, frustration, shame, guilt, and self-pity—same as I do with anyone or anything I want to have a good relationship with.

Diabetes is—like everything else in life—whatever I decide it is. How I experience disease, death, pain, or any circumstance at all depends fully on the meaning I give to it. Now that I know that, I choose my meanings consciously and intentionally to serve me versus hurt me, and I hope you will consider doing the same.

I recognized over time that forgiveness is the most freeing act that one can choose to experience. The sooner I choose forgiveness in any and all situations where I feel any level of tension, the more joy I am able to experience in my life and the more joy I can bring to others.

Face the pain instead of numbing it. Feel the pain. Identify it and take back the power—your power—you've been giving it. Forgive all of it and then let it go. You must stop blaming past or present experiences or circumstances for your life conditions. Forgive them once and for all if you truly want the way you experience life every day to change for the better. Then forgive again. And again. And again. And again. And again. And again.

Dig deep and find out who and/or what you need to forgive, including yourself, and then give yourself one of the greatest gifts that only you can give. Surrender everything you can't change to the Universe or God or Love or Gaia or to complete nothingness. Just let it go.

Just surrender it outside of yourself—release the weight and energy of the pain you've been clinging to because it's familiar and easy to access. Open up space for the unlimited potential you possess to *feel good for no reason* other than that you exist. Once you are willing to do that for yourself, you won't be able to *not* bring more joy to yourself and others in all situations throughout your life.

YOUR STORY PART 4: FORGIVE

"Forgive yourself for not knowing what you didn't know before you learned it."
—Maya Angelou

What lessons have you learned? What thoughts on your story, on your Next Level Life, have started coming up?

Oftentimes at first, people tend to feel angry—incredulous even—when they are prompted to entertain the idea of forgiving someone or something that hurt them (including themselves). Anger is a very valuable sign-post on the roads of our lives. When it pops up, it can be used as a tool to show us things that are keeping us from feeling unburdened by circumstances out of our control.

The saying "holding on to anger is like drinking poison and expecting the other person to die" is so incredibly relevant to our willingness to acknowledge the anger while also beginning to entertain initiating acts of forgiveness into our own lives—no wonder it's such a commonly used quote.

Just saying, "I forgive you," whether aloud or in your head, has the power to set you free in that moment.

Once you *know* that the only person who is being hurt by your unwillingness to forgive all people and circumstances you've been angry at is yourself, forgiveness becomes a bit easier to move forward with as long as you have accepted that you are deserving of endless amounts of love—particularly from yourself.

Forgiveness is an act of self-love done for nobody but yourself so that you can release negativity and dark clouds in order to move forward. Forgiveness means letting go of the illusion of hope for a better past and placing focus on the reality of creating a better future, right now in the present.

These next 3 lessons will help guide you on your path to embracing forgiveness as an ongoing *practice* that will undoubtedly allow you to feel more love, joy, and connection in your life every day.

FORGIVENESS LESSONS INTRO

"When you blame others, you give up your power to change."
—Robert Anthony

What is forgiveness? First and foremost, forgiveness is the cessation of negative energy, negative thoughts and beliefs about a person, situation, subject, circumstance, or even a period of time. It's about intentionally giving up anger and blame toward somebody or something in particular—*including yourself.*

It is fully surrendering your anger and blame to the cosmos in the knowledge that by holding onto it you are only hurting yourself and believing that you cannot change the past, but you can choose to walk the path of clearing the stagnant energy so old wounds can finally have a chance to heal.

We see countless examples of this throughout history—both recent and long ago. One example that stands out to me after learning about it from one of my greatest teachers, Dr. Wayne Dyer, is the story of a woman named Immaculle Ilibagiza. During the Rwandan genocide in the mid-nineties, her entire family was murdered in a massacre.

Her life was spared only because she and seven other women hid in a small bathroom (twelve square feet in size) during the ordeal for ninety-one days. Immaculee chose to openly forgive the people behind the death of her family because she felt strongly that bitterness and hatred would only destroy her from the inside out. She went on to write a bestselling book entitled *Left to Tell* and founded the Left to Tell Charitable Fund in order to help children who have been orphaned due to genocide. Talk about turning adversity into advantage and paying it forward to the greater good of humanity!

There are too many examples of the demonstration of forgiveness spanning all of humanity throughout history for anyone to say anything other than that everyone—every single person in the world—has the full capacity and potential for forgiveness on all levels. This certainly includes you and me.

What we're going to learn today is not only how to put the surrendering portion of the forgiveness equation into action, we're going to plus up our forgiveness. It's something we call Next Level Forgiveness. Let's get started on our first lesson.

FORGIVENESS LESSON 1: FOR YOURSELF

"Forgiveness is the fragrance the violet sheds on the heel that has crushed it."
—Mark Twain

BY DANIELE

When it comes to forgiving yourself for any and all things, I believe that acceptance is the most important thought, word, and action we must embrace. Maybe you embrace acceptance partially at first consideration. However, intentionally working toward full and total surrender to acceptance of all things that ever were, are, and will be is the true path to happiness and peace of mind in all areas of life.

What's done is done, no matter who it was done by, how much it hurt, or how wonderful it felt. That cannot be changed, only accepted. If you choose not to accept all things that have happened in your past, that equals choosing stress, anxiety, and fear, as you will always continue to hold on to some inconceivable and false notion that anything at all about the past could ever be different. It cannot.

The only thing that can change is the meaning you give it and the amount of focus you put on it.

If acceptance of a current circumstance or person in your life is the issue, you have two real options that will guarantee change: you can either change the meaning you have assigned to this circumstance or person, or you can remove yourself from that circumstance or from that person's presence. Those are the only choices that will change your experience of life for the better.

All we have is now. As human beings, we have an unconscious, default tendency to continually re-live past experiences, and for most of us, the experiences we continually re-live are negative ones. When you allow your mind to consistently and habitually wander backward and to continue to feel the emotions you have tied to an experience over and over again—especially when that experience is negative—that is a gigantic roadblock to forgiveness. Doing this is an unconscious decision to repeatedly experience familiar pain that you carry around like a back-breaking chip on your shoulder—because it is deeply ingrained into your being and easy to access, much like any habit.

The only thing we can control that will undoubtedly make all the difference in our lives moving forward regarding true forgiveness of self and others is what we say, do, and act upon *now*. You can choose to turn an experience you once labeled horrifying and life-shattering into an invaluable teacher (and an opportunity to help others) if you choose.

Diabetes didn't happen to me, it happened for me is a prime example of consciously and intentionally choosing a new story—a new meaning.

All the years I spent in pain were based on the meaning I assigned to my circumstance. Diabetes happened *to* me. Why did this happen *to* me? How could this happen *to* me? Why do I have such bad luck? Why can't I catch a break? Why does person X have all the luck and I don't? Anytime you say those words, you are presupposing that you did something wrong, that there is a logical answer to that illogical question. My brain used to give me answers like *It happened to you because you deserve it. Because you're not enough. Because you're defective. Because you're broken. Because you are a bad person.* And on and on and on. All total BS. None of it is based in reality, logic, or reason—these painful answers to these harmful questions are based only on your unconsciously assigned meanings.

USE YOUR BRAIN TO YOUR ADVANTAGE

Your brain will give you answers to whatever questions you ask it, so you must choose to ask different questions to break your old patterns. Try these instead of the ones above and see what your brain comes up with:

- What can I do right now to *practice* self-love?

- What is one thing that I'm grateful for right now and why?
- Who can I help right now?
- What one small action can I take right now that will lead me in the direction of something I'm trying to achieve?

Your brain will do whatever you ask it to—just like any other tool, it is only as effective as its user's willingness to operate it consciously and intentionally. Use it wisely!

You can re-assign meaning to any circumstance, past, or present. You can, at any time, change the word "to" to "for," much like I did with diabetes. It is up to you to assign meaning to every single thing that ever happens to you. This is the best news... You get to choose! You already assign meaning unconsciously every time you have any experience, and I know that once you choose to go from unconsciously assigning meanings to *consciously* assigning meanings, forgiveness becomes a much easier act to implement time and time again.

I eventually had to come to terms with the fact that if I did not forgive myself for all of my past transgressions—all the physical, emotional, and spiritual damage I did to myself over many years due to excessive binge eating, belittling and undervaluing myself, and having little to no care or concern for my own health or well-being, as well as treating others poorly based on my own self-worth—I would never be happy or healthy.

Feeling happy and healthy is *always* on the top of my list of priorities and intentions every day, and one of the most crucial keys to achieving those priorities every day is to accept that forgiveness is a continual *practice*. I don't believe that one day I will wake up and not need to *practice* forgiveness any more. I *am* forgiveness.

Yes, I hurt myself. Yes, I hurt other people. I am human. You are human. There is not one adult alive that has not either hurt themselves and/or other people in the past, or is currently doing it right now, whether consciously or unconsciously. There is no person who is incapable or undeserving of full and total forgiveness if they choose to embrace that path.

One of the things that helped me the most on my path to forgiving myself was the eventual understanding and acceptance of the oneness of everything. I spent the majority of my life walking the line of agnostic–atheist. Over the past ten years or so, I have begun to fully feel the presence of a higher power, and the knowing that that same higher power is inside every one of us.

That same power is nature, the Earth, and the cosmos. Any and all things, living or nonliving, all make up a part of it and are made of the same star stuff. We are all connected; of this I have *zero* doubt.

I do not subscribe to any traditional religious constructs. My challenge with many traditional religious constructs is that at some point in their teachings, they *separate* people instead of uniting us as *humans.*

The power of the Earth and everything that exists on it, a tiny blip in the whole of the cosmos, and the fact that at any moment, anything could happen and all of humanity could cease to exist—yet it continually doesn't—is miraculous enough for me to accept that I don't know what is what, but I do know that we are all in this together no matter what man-made beliefs we allow to separate us.

I have no idea how this all works. I *do know* that my religion is love, my race is human, and my birthplace is Earth. This construct works for any religion, and forgiveness is non-denominational. I am a human and so are you. I see your eyes, your smile, and your heart—I feel your energy no matter what language you speak, what color your skin is, or any other trait that might be visibly different than my own.

This is the only way of life that makes sense to me. This is the only way of existence that feels good to me. And the response I get from every person I interact with continually bolsters this way of life I choose to live. Separation of any kind is created by our minds, and does not truly exist.

Through consistent personal development and the exploration of my feelings, I began to understand that that higher power not only "exists" in nature but *is* nature. We, as human beings, are part of nature and therefore are part of that divinity. We are all part of that higher power—we all possess a little sliver of divinity simply because we exist.

WE ARE ONE

Once we recognize and continually nurture and grow that part of ourselves—through love, forgiveness, and perseverance—the Universe is ecstatic to support our endeavors because they are in alignment with our true selves. We see proof of this support of alignment when we see "coincidences" and synchronicities showing up to meet us where we stand.

We are all cut from the same cloth of the cosmos, of the Universal materials that make up all matter. One of my favorite thought provoking Wayne Dyer queries is, "If you take a bucket of water out of the ocean, is the water in the bucket still part of the ocean as a whole?" My answer is yes, absolutely.

That is how I interpret humanity, existence, and the Universe. No matter what you believe, we're all created the same exact way and of the same exact materials, regardless of whether or not the how or why can be understood, or where our proverbial bucket of the ocean exists.

Once I truly understood and embraced that every single thing and person is fully connected with one another, forgiveness became natural and habitual.

Even the thought of believing I was undeserving of forgiveness became insanity in my own mind; it took quite a bit longer to accept that even those who appear to act in complete opposition to love and forgiveness are playing an important role in waking up the consciousness of humanity. The key is for me to stay in my own power of love and forgiveness while also experiencing negative feelings at the same time—and not for prolonged periods of time. That is where the lessons are hiding.

With the acceptance of oneness, not only did I accept myself, but I accepted everything else that exists in full and total love, knowing that even though these people or circumstances appear in extreme opposition to love, they are there to demonstrate the lesson that living in love, acceptance, and forgiveness means everything in regard to continually working towards solving humanity's challenges.

You may currently have the notion of being unlovable or unforgivable because allowing yourself to feel love or forgiveness in any capacity makes you so uncomfortable. Feeling bad has actually become comfortable and familiar—a habit—a repetitive pattern. The only way to move past that is to break that pattern, forgive yourself, and repeat. Over and over and over again.

Break the pattern. Break the negative thought cycle with gratitude stacking or music or journaling or taking a walk or cuddling with a pet. Breaking old patterns and replacing them with demonstrations of love and forgiveness takes repeated *practice*. There is no easy way out or short cut to changing your patterns. *Practice* forgiving yourself. Act as if you've already forgiven yourself. Try that on and see what it feels like. You deserve it. You are worth it. Never give up.

TAKE ACTION

Take some time to identify any separation beliefs you have about humanity. These could include sex, race, ethnicity, gender, sexual orientation, political affiliation, etc. We all have them at some level, and the only way we can truly begin eradicating them is to identify and acknowledge them so we can consciously move past them.

When I was twenty-one, a boyfriend of mine had a very separatist uncle. I remember being in the car with my boyfriend, his mom, his uncle, and his aunt going to a family function when the uncle made an incredibly derogatory comment about Jewish people, knowing my family associated themselves with the Jewish religion (my maiden name was Shapiro—he was clearly trying to assert his dominance by showing me he thought I was less than he was). Even back then, even not being a religious person, it made me feel sick that this man somehow saw himself as better than any other human being.

It made no sense to me, even back then, even as unawake as I still was, I clearly remember interpreting his egoic expressions as a massive detriment to his character. I took it as a lesson on making sure I never made another human being feel the way he was trying to make me feel—lesser than. I know this happens every single day to all manner of people, and that's why I'm asking you to do this exercise.

Sometimes we do things like this without ever realizing the damage it is doing to the greater good of humanity. The energetic vibration of separating from others and thinking oneself superior to others is detrimental to love, forgiveness, growth, and progress. We are one. Oneness is a concept that takes time and *practice* for most, and I invite you to try it on here, if even for a moment.

Are there any beliefs in your life that are holding you back from acting in a way that demonstrates that you believe all humans deserve to be treated equally? If so, the first step to changing that is to forgive yourself.

FORGIVENESS LESSON 2: FOR OTHERS

"The weak can never forgive. Forgiveness is the attribute of the strong."
— Mahatma Gandhi

BY BILL

We're going to use more forgiveness in our life, not just because it's "the right thing" to do. We're going to implement forgiveness because it is important to us as individuals in improving how we live our lives and how we feel day to day.

And that does not necessarily mean having to wait for them to say they are sorry. As a matter of fact, they may *never* say they're sorry. The whole idea is that you're going to take the power of forgiveness into your own hands and wield it as the powerful tool it is.

Why would this be something that you would want to do? First of all, when you start to identify yourself as a forgiving person, there is immense strength in that, as well as a profound sense of freedom.

Any time you harbor negative emotions and animosity toward somebody, they have power over you, or rather, *you are giving them power over you*. Whether they know they have power over you or not, you are letting your thoughts and your feelings for that individual control how you live your life and what actions you take.

By forgiving them, you're saying, "I no longer give you the power to control how I feel in this moment." It frees you up mentally, physically, and spiritually and empowers you like nothing else can.

With great power comes great responsibility, meaning if you're freed from your negative emotions, you can focus that energy on other things. Ideally, you will focus your efforts on realizing your life's purpose and acting on your personal mission. (We'll go into more depth on your life's purpose in a later lesson.)

For now, one important thing to keep in mind is that people do whatever they do for their own reasons. It can make it easier to be forgiving if you recognize this fact. What they did that affected you could have been accidental or on purpose, but either way, it wasn't about you, it was about them—a reflection of themselves. They might have a repetitive pattern of destructive behavior that hurt you, or are in so much pain themselves that pain is all they know.

Whatever the reason, that's the best that they could do with what they had at that moment.

You cannot control their actions, but you can control your actions. Your job is to become the most loving, forgiving *you* that you can be in any given situation. By recognizing that they're doing the best they can with the resources they have at the time, it frees you from the burden of blaming them.

In addition, we never want to forget the reason we're in pain or are feeling betrayed, hurt, misled—whatever feeling that's eliciting the need for forgiveness that we're feeling in any given situation, so that we can use it as a teacher in the future to avoid repeating the same pattern again.

I do want to stress that if you're ever in a situation where you feel unsafe or your physical well-being is in danger, then holding that anger, holding that grudge might be something that is good if it gets you to safety, if it gets you out of a certain situation. When it comes to the safety and security of you and your loved ones, take whatever safe actions you can to ensure that you're not putting yourself in harm's way.

HOW TO FORGIVE

Forgiveness is a thought, a feeling, and a behavior. And the good news is that you can train and *practice* forgiveness until it becomes a habit—second nature.

If you only *practice* forgiveness at the level of thought by thinking "I forgive you," for instance, without acknowledging the feelings of anger and the process of letting it go—of surrender and release—then your *practice* will be less impactful than if you include the other aspects involved in the process.

You don't have to get it perfect. Thinking the words in your mind is a great first step that will get you moving in the right direction.

The next step is saying the words aloud, even just to yourself. Say the words, "I forgive you" right now. Even if you didn't have anyone in mind, it is likely that you felt a subtle shift in your emotions—maybe you even felt your body take in a deep breath and relax a little more.

That's because when we say the words aloud, we're going beyond the thought into the realm of behavior, and when we say the words and hear ourselves say them, it stirs the emotions inside of us.

After saying the words out loud, we want to move forward and actively include our feelings and emotions to make our forgiveness *practices* more complete.

One guiding emotion that will help you in your forgiveness *practice* is anger. Anger can be used as a map to help you figure out what's really going on behind the scenes in your own head.

Oftentimes anger can be linked to our healthy boundaries. When someone breaks our internally set rules—our personal blueprint of how life *should* be—disrespects us or says something that offends us, our anger is a way of getting our bodies and minds ready to defend and protect ourselves.

We can see then why anger can be so addicting. It makes us feel powerful, and then we associate being angry with having control over a situation. That often leads to holding on to that anger-fueled power, which can turn into resolute resentment and negativity over time. No wonder it can feel so hard to forgive.

The lesson here is that forgiveness is for the strong, not the weak. It's a potent *practice* to engage in if it's lasting peace that you seek. Because by forgiving, you are saying to yourself and the world that it's not anger that makes you strong, instead it is your life force, your love, purpose, faith, and character that make you truly powerful.

In our Next Level Forgiveness *practice,* we only want to use anger as a temporary tool because holding a grudge, holding on to negative feelings can harm us, but we don't necessarily want to forget the reason that we were in that negative state, particularly so we don't repeat it.

What we're going to do is *practice* forgiving. The first step is to think of a situation or a person that you are holding onto resentment for: a family member, coworker, erratic driver, or even yourself.

Then, summon up your courage and your feelings of love. You can do this by thinking about and feeling the love you have for yourself, for a loved one, Earth, God, or use the gratitude stacking *practice* you learned earlier in the Love Lesson.

Once you feel full of love, shift your focus back to an image of that person or situation that you are holding onto resentment for in your mind. Allow yourself to recall and feel the emotions that are causing you to hold onto anger. You don't have to relive it second by second, just bring up the incident or circumstance, and acknowledge it mentally or by saying the words, "I accept that this has happened, but I won't let this circumstance control me and the quality of my life."

Then say aloud, "I forgive you."

Visualize the red-hot anger fade away and be replaced by the light of love that you have been building. This light can be a pink, blue, green, yellow, white, or any color that makes you feel calm and loving.

NEXT LEVEL FORGIVENESS

Demonstrating forgiveness in the ways described above feels good—much better than the searing anger and resentment that were festering before. Now we're going to implement Next Level Forgiveness. Instead of simply ceasing to feel negativity, you are going to send love and positivity in the direction of the person you just forgave.

Forgive, then send love! Send blessings and positive vibes. It shifts everything toward the direction of love.

Depending on the severity of the situation and the relationship between yourself and the forgiven, you can send positive energy, blessings, and/or love. The means by which you send your positive energy will be determined by your current mental, emotional, and spiritual *practices*, but the outcomes are the same. You will no longer feel anger (or at least you will feel less anger) and instead you will replace it with love.

It gamifies the forgiveness process when you start asking, *"How fast can I turn resentment into joy?"*

It turns it from a game of suffering, into a game of giving. Instead of just forgiving and ceasing anger, you are "for" "giving" of positive energy. This is what we mean by Next Level Forgiveness. It's quite literally a game changer!

It becomes pretty easy once you get the hang of it and develop the habit since you only have to say it to yourself, and it feels pretty darn good to do so.

You don't have to say any of this to the person at all. This makes it possible to forgive people who are no longer alive or ones that you don't want to get into a confrontation with. If you couldn't do it this way, you would hold grudges without any hope of recovery.

It took me years in my own situation to forgive my brother after the mental institution because I was, without realizing it, waiting for an apology. I've now taken my forgiveness *practice* to a new level. I don't need to wait for the apology. I can just forgive anytime I need to, and that vastly improves the quality of my life overall—that's really what we're looking for.

The final point in this chapter on forgiveness is that now that you've freed up negative energy that you were holding on to—now that you've cleared the cluttered spaces in your mind, body, and spirit—you now have more energy to focus on your goals and purpose. The more you forgive, the more focus you are able to place on what's really important to you.

TAKE ACTION

We're going to do some forgiveness affirmations, which are simply declarations of your intended purpose or outcome. You can either say them out loud, think them in your mind, or, preferably, write them down *and* say them out loud. Write down ten times in your journal, "I am forgiving and forgivable." This is very similar to our "I am loving and lovable," affirmations you did in the love section. Then read those words aloud ten times. For bonus points, you can make this part of your daily *Love, Forgive, Never Give Up practice*.

By remembering that you are forgivable, you can forgive yourself as often as needed. In addition, forgiving yourself opens the energetic door for others to forgive you, and you can forgive them more easily as well. Each time you say or write those words, it will reinforce what you are learning today and the desired outcome of feeling unburdened by carrying around the heaviness of anger and resentment.

The second action item is to think of five people you feel you have wronged at some point in your life. Write this in your journal, then say it out loud. Just say, "I'm sorry. I'm sorry, Dad, for XYZ. I'm sorry, Mark, my friend from college, because of XYZ. I did something that you didn't know about... Or that you did know about." For each of these people, write, "I am sorry" for whatever it is you feel guilty for and then why you are sorry.

If you feel inspired, call this person and apologize, or write them a letter regardless of intent to send it. That works well, too. But the idea is to feel it *inside you* first. When you accept the fact that you can say you're sorry to other people, it opens you up to the idea that all people are *worthy* of forgiveness.

Your third action item is to *practice* forgiveness using the technique in the HOW TO FORGIVE section. If you already walked through the practice with someone specific in mind, you can choose to practice with someone else, or using the same person which will both help you get better at the practice and really lock it in. The point is to *practice* it and really work on it until it becomes a habit. *You might want to add a bookmark to that page so you can easily come back to it again and again.*

FORGIVENESS LESSON 3: FOR THE WORLD

"The practice of forgiveness is our most important contribution to the healing of the world."
—Marianne Williamson

We've come a long way already from self-forgiveness, learning to let go of blame, and refusing to beat ourselves up anymore for things that we cannot change. Now it's time to take that same energy and apply it toward making a better life for ourselves and those we love.

Using Next Level Forgiveness is not just the cessation of negative thoughts toward others, not just no longer blaming or being angry—we're using Next Level Forgiveness in order to generate, emit, and share positive energy. We're taking it a step further and sending love and goodwill to those we are forgiving. In doing so, we're increasing the ever-upward cycle of positivity. A virtuous cycle, if you will.

Now we're going to hold the vision for what it would look like to live in a world that had more forgiveness. When we develop our powers of forgiveness, we possess a level of focus that has the ability to heal. Once again, we demonstrate the possibilities. Others see our example and are open to making changes in their own lives in the same way we are demonstrating.

In many ways, forgiveness truly is the path to world peace. Many world-level challenges are fueled by holding on to deeply ingrained wrongs from generations, using pride or not wanting to seem weak as an excuse or a crutch. We've already learned that practicing forgiveness equals strength. Only the strong can forgive. If we are willing to learn to forgive and demonstrate that it's *possible* to forgive, we set the stage for a world that is at peace with itself.

It's an incredible challenge, but it's also incredibly inspiring and empowering to know that the best thing that you can do to enact that change is to start with yourself. Take those steps to be more forgiving in your life right now. Remember, "we" starts with "me."

TAKE ACTION

For your action item, we're going to have a creative, fun thought process. What if everybody on the planet had twice the level of forgiveness in them?

Imagine if everybody was forgiving and also had the capacity to send goodwill to those who wronged them. What would that look and feel like in regards to your family? What would that look and feel like in your town? What would that look and feel like at the national level? At the global level?

Paint a picture of what it would look like if, overnight, everyone woke up and was overwhelmed with the spirit of forgiveness that we've learned is incomprehensibly powerful and impactful. Paint that picture, breathe life into it, and let's see if we can *live it* just a little bit more.

HERO'S QUEST: FORGIVE

"Dumbledore says people find it far easier to forgive others for being wrong than being right."
—Hermione Granger, *Harry Potter and the Half-Blood Prince*, J.K. Rowling

The path through the twisted forest was fraught with more dangers and risks than you had anticipated. Along the way, the reflecting mirrors of the trials of truth revealed to you thoughts you did not know you had—though with them in the open, you were able face and overcome them.

And through it all... you arose victorious! Your prize is the Orb of Forgiveness.

The Orb of Forgiveness glows green and grows warm as you feel the healing and focus seep into you. You feel a surge of strength as you raise your head a little taller, roll back your shoulders, raise your chin, release negative feelings, and project positive ones instead.

The Orb of Forgiveness now in hand and the Shield of Love upon your back, you consult the magical tome in your hands. A new map appears, showing you the way up the dark, lava-strewn peaks of the Mountain of Woe.

Soon you will make that dangerous climb, test your mettle in the trials of courage, and come face to face with death itself... With the Sword of Perseverance as the prize to be won!

Adventure on to discover what you must do to harness your true powers of love and forgiveness.

The Zen masters say, "When you're ready to learn you must empty your cup."

Now turn the page and:

NEVER GIVE UP!

BILL'S STORY: NEVER GIVE UP!

THEN

I woke up the day after my 22nd birthday in a bed in my parents' home. I moved back in with them the year before, after I came to terms with myself through love and forgiveness. Now I wanted to finish my schooling, and I wanted my family to come together and heal in order for us to have a real, genuine, authentic connection—without any masks of deception this time.

My parents wanted that as well, and within a few weeks of our conversation about it, my dad made the 6-hour drive out to Pittsburgh in his truck with an open-air trailer in tow. We loaded up all of my belongings, and just like when I left the mental institution a decade earlier, my father took me home again.

I took classes at the local community college, setting myself up to transfer to a university for an environmental science degree since I had decided I wanted to work on doing something that would help change the world for the better. I worked a full-time job at the gym and biked everywhere, all the while getting reacquainted with my family and learning to be with them in a new way.

Things were going pretty good until the morning after my birthday.

That day was September 11, 2001.

My mom called me down to watch the devastation on the news, and when I watched the towers fall, something inside me snapped.

I had been so focused on me—my wants and my recovery—that I wasn't in a position to do anything about what was happening 100 miles to the north in New York City. I went downstairs to the basement, and I punched the punching bag with rage as the tears fell.

I felt helpless. *Hopeless.* Unable to do anything. Something inside me rose up. It was the same voice I had heard many times growing up while going through my tough times. This time, I wanted to do something to help others, not just myself.

More than that, in my heart, mind, and soul, I had come to believe that the strong have a duty to help those who need it most.

A week later, I joined the Army National Guard. A year later, I completed basic training and advanced individual training as a 25B, Information Systems Operator. 2 years later, I found myself on a C130 troop transport plane flying from Kuwait to Tikrit, Iraq, along with the 42nd Infantry Division—the first division-level reserve element activated since World War II.

***

We landed at Forward Operating Base Danger, which was Saddam Hussein's walled-in, summertime palatial compound turned into a military operating base. All around the base, miniature castles that had been given as gifts to friends and military leaders in Saddam's regime were converted into company command-level elements. The primary HQ building was a massive palace that stood atop a bluff overlooking the Tigris River and flat plains for miles in every direction.

And just as far we could see, so too could we be seen. We were subject to a nearly continuous stream of incoming mortar rounds. Luckily, about half were duds.

The temperature in January when we arrived was cool during the day and freezing at night, but during the summer months, with the sun beating down and clear skies overhead, it regularly reached 120 degrees or higher. When we were on task around the operating base, we wore our body armor and carried assault rifles and any gear that was needed, increasing the temperatures dramatically.

Though my personal views on why we were fighting in Iraq didn't match up with why we were there, I took this experience as an opportunity to serve my country—to serve something higher than myself—and once I had reconciled that with myself, I was all-in.

I trained with the Army in network operations. Essentially, I assisted in the mission of keeping up the military network for an area the size of Texas. I was qualified, skilled, and ready to make a difference from day one.

There was just one problem.

Believe it or not, sometimes in a large government run organization, paperwork gets messed up or lost, and my promotion to the rank of specialist was not recognized.

That was not good.

In fact, I was now the lowest ranking soldier in my unit.

That was even worse!

And since the military is an hierarchal organization, they would often set the lowest ranking individual on the lowest value task despite their qualifications.

It didn't help that there was a master sergeant in charge of our group who reveled in assigning me these low-value tasks. "Hargenrader! Grab a broom!" "Hargenrader! Grab a rag!" I could quickly see that my yearlong tour was going from one of meaningful service and exceptional value to one of menial labor.

I was thousands of miles away from home, working 13 hour shifts, 7 days a week, with a leader who was assigning me cleaning detail versus designing, implementing, configuring, and operating networks.

It was then that I heard that familiar voice in my head that said, "I will figure this out."

Instead of feeling sorry for myself and with a grin on my face, I was now engaged in finding a way to solve this challenge.

Shortly after that, I happened upon my opportunity. It was a long shot, and there were some risks involved. But I put my plan into action nonetheless.

Here's how it went down.

When we took over network operations from 1st Infantry Division, the Big Red 1, we performed what's called a left seat, right seat ride. For one week, we each shadowed the solider who was performing the job we were taking over for—learning from them about how they did it. Then, for another week, we performed the job while they watched and gave pointers. After that, they left, and we were on our own.

I got my eyes on the master job list spreadsheet and saw that my name was penciled in at the lowest job on the roster: accepting and signing for equipment and laptops when they were turned in for repair.

That was not the job I wanted.

Simultaneously, I noticed that there was a blank space several rows and ranks up, next to a staff sergeant whose job responsibilities included configuring switches and routers, setting up wireless internet shots across the base, and administrating a coalition forces network.

Now *that* was the job I wanted! Something that would push me and add real value to the mission.

And through the magic of pencils and erasers, I was *miraculously* paired up with that staff sergeant! (Sergeant Evans from the 1st ID, if you're reading this, drop me a line!)

I was immediately turned away by that sergeant. He didn't think I would have the skills to take over. That was why no one had been paired with him in the first place. I convinced him to let me try, and the next 2 weeks were some of the hardest and longest hours I have ever worked in my life.

I learned from the sergeant during the day and would stay up most of the night learning the router commands, practicing on simulators, sometimes pulling out a cot to rest my eyes and to catch a few hours of sleep instead of heading back to the barracks with the rest of the day shift unit while the night shift took over.

Then in the morning when the sergeant returned, I showed him what I had learned and what I could do. He would nod his approval then quickly show me some other incredibly complicated and complex computing equipment configuration protocol I had no idea how to complete, and so the process would start over again.

Finally, at the end of the 2 weeks, although I was exhausted, I had earned his official approval to take over his duties. With a handshake, he was gone along with the rest of the 1st Infantry Division.

We were on our own, and I was ready to serve at the highest level of my abilities.

Shortly after we took over, the master sergeant called to me, "Hargenrader! Where've you been? We've got cleaning detail for you."

I replied, "Master sergeant, I'd love to assist in that effort, but I've been tasked with reconfiguring the wireless network, and that will take me all day."

A smart, bold, and no-nonsense warrant officer quickly stepped in and confirmed that I was indeed not allowed to be removed from this mission-critical task. The look on the master sergeant's face was priceless!

Even though I wasn't punching bullies in the face anymore, let's just say I was still finding ways to push back at those who would use their power to intimidate and antagonize others.

The year went quickly in some ways and slowly in others. I worked long hours, worked out, and even took online college courses while I was in the war zone (one of the benefits of being in charge of the internet connections). And then it was time for us to pack up our equipment. We were the last unit to leave Forward Operating Base Danger.

I can still see the dual-rotor troop carrier Chinook helicopter landing. I can feel the hot air on my face as we loaded up through the opening in the back and strapped in for takeoff. I looked out the open bay door as we took off and watched as the base I had called home for the last 11 months receded off into the distance.

Not everyone made it back alive. Gratefully, I did. I was going home.

My globe hopping in the military helped me realize that I wanted to travel more. Shortly after I returned home, I took a trip with my second-youngest brother to the white sand beaches of Cancun. While in Mexico, I met my then future wife Daniele. That's a story I'll save for another day!

NOW

Regarding the lessons of perseverance in this chapter of my life, there are many. As we progress in life, our aims become less about how we can help ourselves and more about how we can help others. We can use the same skills, tools, and tactics, but now, we can affect greater change.

A never-give-up attitude means we won't settle for less, and when we are dealt a bad hand—like a paperwork mistake reducing us in rank—we don't throw in the towel!

At that stage in my life I still hadn't honed in on what my true purpose was, but I was determined to discover it, create it, cultivate it, and focus in on it. And because I had that goal in mind, I was able to make it through some of my toughest challenges in life.

In a synchronistic example of life imitates art, I read from the pages of the *Chronicles of the Warrior Lost* after William had escaped his captors:

My new training grounds have been found... I am not close to what I once was but my mind has changed too. It was never in me to hurt the innocent even when I didn't rightly know what innocence was. But it is in me to punish the evil and this I will do. I am the warrior...

I've now come to realize that we don't need to fight in a war to embody the heart, courage, and passion of the warrior. The world needs more Peaceful Warriors, Love Warriors, Next Level Life Warriors, and many other INSERT CAUSE HERE Warriors.

At its core, a warrior is a person engaged in some struggle or conflict, and there are plenty of struggles that we have to face in our own lives, as well as on a broader humanitarian scale.

While there still exists a real need for protectors that wear the uniform—and I honor those who have come before me and still fight for freedom to this day—when we look at the world as a whole and the peaceful progress we've made, it's not a far stretch to say that someday we can live in a world without war.

That's not a fantasy world without disagreement, tragedy, or struggle, but it is a world where instead of putting our collective mind-power, energy, and funding toward warfare, we instead spend it on bettering the lives of those around us, feeding humanity, ensuring those who need medical help get it without crippling, inconceivable costs, protecting the planet and its inhabitants (ourselves included), making even more progress in scientific endeavors, including developing more cures for disease, deploying affordable clean energy globally, and colonizing the Moon, Mars, and beyond.

Lasting peace is within our reach. That's a belief I will never give up on.

We'll go over more Never Give Up tools, tactics, and techniques in greater detail later, but for now, let's check in with Daniele.

DANIELE'S STORY: NEVER GIVE UP!

"When we are no longer able to change a situation, we are challenged to change ourselves."
—Viktor Frankl

Have you ever walked across more than six feet in length of burning hot coals? Coals that were literally on fire—burning so brightly that they were white hot and smoking, so intense that it made you sweat just to stand near them?

I have done this thing that some consider insane three times so far in my life. The first time in 2009, most recently in 2013, and it is likely that I'll do it again. I have done it once alongside Bill, once with my best friend, and once with my mom (yes, my sixty-something-year-old mom walked across burning coals—she is my hero).

Just in case you want to walk on coals (and have an all-around incredible, life-changing personal development experience), please be smart about it. I recommend doing it the way my family and I did, which was at an event supervised by experienced professionals called Unleash the Power Within hosted by Tony Robbins. Google it. Go to it. You won't regret it!

Each time, we were in the company of thousands of other people whom we had never met before, all of us excited and freaking out while waiting for our turn to step up to face the fears that, up until that point, had been holding us back in our lives.

Each time I took off my shoes and socks, rolled up my pant legs, regulated my breathing, repeated my mantra, and trusted in the process that millions of others had successfully gone through before me, I was demonstrating something to the Universe and to myself (I believe we are one in the same). With this action, backed by faith, I was now and would continue to remain ready to step forward, to step up, to persevere through any and all manner of challenge that life would inevitably place on my path.

I was always naturally perseverant. Even when I didn't feel a desire to push through a challenging situation, I always ended up doing so anyway—whether quickly or painfully slowly. I credit this to my most influential role models, my parents, particularly my mom.

Humans model and emulate who and what we pay attention to and spend time around the most and what gives us feedback the most (positive or negative). I was blessed to grow up with some of the strongest, smartest, most loving human beings as parents who always showed me that they believed in our ability to figure anything out.

My mom has effectively dealt with the early and unexpected deaths of just about every person she has ever loved. Her father died young, well before I was born. Her mother died just six months before I was born. The love of her life, her husband of twenty-two years and my father. Her only sister, my aunt, died in 2000 from a long battle with cancer. Her step-daughter, my sister, died after a life of addiction in 2008. Not to mention all the other trials and tribulations life dealt her, the least of which was raising a daughter with type 1 diabetes.

I watched her deal with all of this seemingly insurmountable, heart-wrenching loss with the grace of love and forgiveness she always naturally possessed. She most certainly never gave up. She is and always has been the kindest, wisest, empathetic and most loving, even-keeled, generous, easy-going, and humorous human being I have ever witnessed in my life. She is why I am.

WE ARE FAMILY—I GOT ALL MY SISTERS WITH ME

My dad had two daughters from his previous marriage before meeting my mom. Both were old enough to have been my mother. However, we always operated as a family unit, and I was not taught any separation in the way of "half" sisters or anything of that nature.

My mom and my sisters were very close. I was always closest to the younger of my two sisters, as she lived in the apartment below us in the duplex my parents built from the ground up and called home. I thought she was so cool. She had a big stereo and would always let me listen to her cassettes, try on her makeup and clothes, or do anything else I wanted to do. And when I was little, what I wanted to do most was spend as much time downstairs in her apartment with her as I could. She was 17 years older than me, yet we always had a very deep connection.

Once I was about six years old, I began to understand things about my sister that I now know my parents were trying to keep off my radar. Very long story short, my sister was a highly functioning heroin addict for the vast majority of her life, on top of experiencing a variety of mental health challenges. She was a successful phlebotomist (she chose to become an expert and build her career around the area of the body she abused: her veins), and she was an incredibly generous and caring woman. As long as she had heroin or methadone, she was a functional member of society.

But, as anyone who has ever loved someone who has suffered from addiction knows, things aren't always functional. As I got older, I noticed and processed more. I remember a time when she begged my dad to handcuff her to her bed and watch over so that she could detox. One time, while searching through an old box of stuff in our basement, I found a letter she wrote and signed granting permission to my dad to restrain her. She wanted out of that life; she just never made it.

I remember hearing the screams coming from the apartment downstairs as her body went through the withdrawal process. I don't remember much else, but I do know that their efforts didn't last.

When I was eighteen, in the year 2000, my sister got a liver transplant due to having advanced cirrhosis and hepatitis C. She passed away in 2008, never able to fully escape her demons and certainly not because of a lack of perseverance. She was one of the most repeatedly kicked-down (often kicked by herself) but never-give-up people I've ever known.

Through all of this, she did something particularly miraculous. She created my nephew. He was born a couple weeks after my twelfth birthday. There was a hell of a lot going on around my twelfth birthday.

First, my dad died. Then, a couple weeks later, my nephew was born. It was so incredibly bittersweet. My dad had three daughters and one granddaughter and would never get the chance to meet his only grandson. My sister had to be pulled away from my dad's coffin at his funeral, screaming and crying, just weeks away from giving birth to her first and only child.

My nephew is now twenty-three years old, and the way he chooses to participate in life never ceases to amaze me. Through growing up with a mother who was always addicted, losing her when he was fourteen, never having a father figure present in his life, and so much more, he has consciously chosen what he wants out of life by using his experiences and what he has observed throughout his life to show him what he does *not* want. He is a successful electrician and a natural-born entrepreneur. He is incredibly smart and, due to his hardships, wise beyond his years. I'm grateful to be his aunt.

ORDER OF OPERATIONS

There is a reason we chose to put love, forgiveness, and never giving up in that particular order. It's like math class. There are orders of operations you are taught to follow to ensure you come up with the best answer—if you choose to never give up *before* you choose to learn how to love and forgive, the outcome could be devastating.

I experienced this firsthand throughout my teenage life, as I was always persevering at beating myself up, calling myself horrible names, blaming myself for things that were out of my control, and staying stagnant in my personal development (mental, physical, and spiritual) due to allowing myself to be crippled by fear or of the unknown, of failure, of rejection, or of not being perfect.

I was also afraid something would compromise my "comfortable" situation, but, looking back now, I was so incredibly, painfully uncomfortable every single day. I associated more pain with the efforts it would take to change than the pain

I associated with staying stuck in my current circumstances, so I persevered at staying the same for a very long time.

I was dedicated to persevering at beating myself down and holding myself back. I was unwilling to give up on anger, hurt, fear, blame, shame, guilt, anxiety, and hopelessness—all of those emotional states are ones that I vow to never persevere at again.

I know that many people are currently stuck in that same purgatory. Wanting to change but associating more pain with the process of change than with staying where they are. It's a bitch of a place to be, and, like the act of forgiveness, *you* are the only one who can do anything about it.

So, with that in mind, is there anything that isn't serving you that you have been persevering at? Is there anything you have not given up on yet—something that, if you chose to give up on, would open up a channel for the light of love and forgiveness to shine through? Negative self-talk? Beliefs that you are not loving or lovable or worthy of love?

YOUR STORY PART 5: NEVER GIVE UP!

"Fear knocked on the door. Faith answered. No one was there."
—English Proverb

What lessons have you learned? What thoughts on your own story, on your Next Level Life have started coming up?

Do you think of yourself as a naturally perseverant person, or do you label yourself as someone who gives up easily? If you're reading this, you've clearly made it through all of the challenges in your life up until now, and that's pretty incredible.

We can all think of times in our own lives where we *had to* persevere—we chose not to give up—through trials and tribulations we never thought we could make it through.

When I think of all of the experiences Bill and I have persevered through—both before we met and through our almost eleven years of marriage that made us stronger, wiser, more conscious and connected—we feel a sense of empowerment, strength, gratitude, and awe for what the human spirit can create out of seemingly hopeless circumstances.

Those are the emotions Bill and I choose to focus on when new challenges inevitably arise, as we know from previous experiences that meeting these challenges with the we-can-figure-this-out mindset of perseverance, that whatever comes of the experience, the lessons will serve us throughout the rest of our lives.

Sometimes it's easier to persevere for someone else—to lead by example because you want that person to see what is possible. Other times, staying the course to prove to yourself what you know you can do can be a major source of motivation. Both are incredibly effective ways to stay focused on *the light that is always inside you* and at the end of the proverbial tunnel (it's there even if you can't see it).

Whenever I need a reminder of what horrors the human spirit can withstand and still come out on the other side in a place of pure, unbounded love, forgiveness, perseverance, and a burning desire to help others do the same, I turn to examples like Nelson Mandela, Viktor Frankl, Immaculée Ilibagiza, and Anne Frank just to name a few, and I recommend you do the same.

Turning to the inspirational energy of other human experiences can be a massively effective fuel for our own ability to believe in our inner wisdom's ability to guide us through the chaos of any storm. They demonstrate possibility—I can't tell you how many times any number of my successes started with me saying *If he/she can do it, I can do it too!*

These next 3 lessons will help guide you on your path toward knowing without a doubt that there is nothing put on your path that you cannot forgive and make peace with.

NEVER GIVE UP LESSONS INTRO

"It's not failure itself that holds you back. It is the fear of failure that paralyzes you."
—Brian Tracy

The main theme of this section is to never give up on being your best self and embracing that you have all that you need to do anything you want inside you at all times—a self whose characteristics, values, and focuses can only be defined by you. That's the only thing you can truly control in your life—your thoughts, your focus, your actions, your language, and the meaning you make out of all things.

A great definition of perseverance is steadfastness in doing something despite difficulty, failures, temporary defeats, and a delay in achieving success.

When you have a purpose in life, it makes the idea of persevering more meaningful because we have something to strive for that is both of ourselves and outside of ourselves. It creates a natural pull, as if being drawn forward toward something versus being focused on just our current situation. We're going to touch more on persistence and purpose in the lessons that follow.

For now, it's important for you to realize that failure is part of life. It's even built into the definition of perseverance. Sometimes in life we can be afraid to fail and so we don't even try.

But that's a self-defeating mindset from the start. We all fail—how we assign meaning to and handle that failure is what determines our level of perseverance in any situation. You can only grow from struggle and stretching outside of your comfort zones, and failure is a tool in your next-level perseverance tool belt.

In a next-level thinking paradigm, you can even find gratitude in your failures when you intend to do so—gratitude for your willingness to try, gratitude for being courageous and acting even though fear is present, gratitude for the lessons learned.

Action-oriented optimism, married with a heaping serving of faith leads to never giving up. The first lesson is to fail forward, meaning that failure is not the end, it's just a step on the journey. You can't fail forward if you don't move at all.

For instance, in martial arts—Brazilian jiu-jitsu in particular—one of the first things you learn is how to fall. Not how to kick, punch, or choke someone out. First, you must learn how to fall, because you're going to get thrown around. You're going to get picked up and dropped forcefully. We learn how to fall so that we can continue to get back up and keep moving and fighting.

Now that you know that it is okay to fail, that failing means you are trying, that you must fail to make progress, and not to let the fear of failure dictate your actions, let's move on to the important lessons on never, ever giving up on yourself.

NEVER GIVE UP LESSON 1: FOR YOURSELF

"I merely took the energy it takes to pout and wrote some blues."
—Duke Ellington

BY DANIELE

When it comes to perseverance, or never completely giving up, it is my belief that there are only two options we can choose that will make a real, true difference in our ability to stay the course through any adversity. We can either change our circumstances or we can change the meanings we assign to our circumstances. Anything else is choosing to feel out of alignment with joy.

To make it through tough times, the actions—*practices*—involved in accepting love and forgiveness in all of your decision-making processes allows you to push through more quickly and effectively in any situation.

Of course, we can and often do choose to do nothing, remaining stagnant. Doing nothing when you are unhappy with any of life's circumstances is also a choice. There are questions we need to ask ourselves when we are in situations that make us unhappy or cause us pain.

"What can I do right now to change (insert circumstance here) that is making me unhappy?" is one of the best questions you can ask if you are able to change the circumstance. Fill in the specific circumstance that is causing you pain. Write it down and see what comes out, dismissing any internal judgement.

If you are unable or unwilling to change the circumstance (a good example would be living with a chronic disease for which there is currently no cure—that is a circumstance one cannot change) you must choose to change your meanings versus changing your circumstances.

A good place to start is, *"What must I do to fully accept and embrace (insert circumstance here)? What new meaning or story must I assign to (insert circumstances here) in order to love them, forgive them, and accept them?"*

Any other questions you ask yourself about circumstances (people, events, or past or current experiences) must not involve any language regarding *why* they occurred or *who* is to blame. Focus on, *"What must I do to change and/or accept this?"* Then, take action on the answer—the sooner the better, no matter how big or small the action is.

Ask yourself, *"What meanings must I assign to (insert circumstance here) to accept them, love them, forgive them, and feel confident that I can keep moving forward toward what is most important to me in life?"* Those are the only questions that matter when it comes to taking control of your choices—your life—and shaping it into what you do want instead of what you don't.

Perseverance is all about perspective. Wayne Dyer famously said, "When we change the way we look at things, the things we look at change." This is a profoundly truth-filled statement. Your perspective, or the way you choose to interpret everything you experience, either allows you to persevere or drags you down to the level of fear. Perspective always drives performance.

I had different perspectives about myself and life in general when I was living in an extremely negative mindset. Some of these perspectives I changed through deep reflection and personal development—exercises and *practices* repeated over and over again.

One of these exercises took place at a personal development seminar almost ten years ago. We were in large groups of about thirty strangers being led by a team leader, and the exercise was based on acknowledging what you consider to be the biggest challenge in your life—the biggest thing holding you back from moving forward and becoming the person you wanted to be.

I had identified that challenge as diabetes. The leader of our team, Chuck, kept asking me over and over again, *"What is diabetes?"* I kept answering, *"It's a disease. It is a dysfunction of the human body. It's a glitch in the matrix. It's a punishment. It is a heavy weight that drags me down."*

No matter how many times I answered, Chuck kept asking me, *"What is diabetes?"* After what seemed like hours but realistically was probably about ten minutes of this intense back-and-forth stream of consciousness where no time was given for deep thought, the words I was using started to change. One of the times he asked me, *"What is diabetes?"* I said, *"It's something that happened to me that will stay with me forever that I have no explanation for."*

The last time he asked the question, the words *"Diabetes happened for me"* just came out. *"Diabetes didn't happen to me. Diabetes happened for me."*

Chuck stopped asking me the question after that answer. Through his extensive training and experience in facilitating the re-conditioning of negative experiences into ones that gave people's perceived suffering true meaning, he knew that it was the answer I needed. During that exercise, he never said any words to me other than *"What is diabetes?"* and that literally changed my life forever.

Once I said those words, my entire life energy shifted. I started crying uncontrollably. I felt like a gigantic weight had been lifted off of my shoulders. I felt a sense of lightness I had never felt before in my life. In that moment, I was unburdened by diabetes for the very first time in more than almost twenty years. I saw the lessons the pain taught me as clear as day. I felt the strength it gifted to me. I was free. Diabetes didn't happen to me. Diabetes happened for me.

That one tiny substitute of the word "to" to "for" changed everything. All of a sudden, my entire life was different. I felt a sense of relief that is extraordinarily difficult to put into words. I had never experienced anything like it.

Simply put, I felt *so much better.* That one little perspective shift changed everything.

I went from persevering while struggling and suffering, to persevering without the burden of struggling and suffering. *Big difference.*

I "GET TO" VERSUS I "HAVE TO"

The other language mindset shift that changed my life and my perspective on perseverance was the "have to" versus "get to" perspective. I bring this back to diabetes because managing this chronic disease is a big part of all aspects of my life.

Not only is it a disease that I have; it is also the career I have chosen. As a facilitator of healing and embracing wholeness through love and forgiveness—an author, speaker, coach, consultant, advocate, nutritionist, personal trainer, and more—I help other people learn how to choose a path of healing and self-care regardless of circumstance and how to leave victimhood behind for good.

I eventually realized that *everything* is a choice, and my choices were the only thing I had control over.

Every single thing you do or don't do is a choice. Every. Single. Thing. Getting out of bed in the morning is a choice, brushing your teeth is a choice—and *not* doing those things are also choices.

I don't have to take my insulin. Nobody is standing next to me holding a gun to my head and saying, "Take your insulin so you can stay alive." I *get to* take my insulin. I get to check my blood sugar. I get to do these things to care for, love, and respect myself, and to persevere through the cards that life dealt me with gratitude in my heart.

As an exercise to bring me back to the mindset of perseverance, I intentionally and temporarily shift my mindset to the perspective of what it would be like *not* to get to do these things. If I am ever feeling any type of self-pity or feeling like I can't push through, I remind myself that there are so many people in the world who need life-saving medications for diseases, and many of them don't *get to* have these medications. There were times in my life when I struggled to afford my insulin and other medical supplies. I know how gut-wrenching a situation like that is. I *get to* have what I need for now, and that is a true blessing.

If you are reading this book, there are probably hundreds of things that you *get to* do every single day that a large portion of the world does not get to do. These are things that, if you did not get to do them, your life would be immeasurably worse in just about all aspects, and that without them you would have to dig down for a level of perseverance you may not have experienced before.

Things like eating, drinking clean water, showering, sleeping in a bed, wearing clothes and shoes that fit, having an education, having internet access, having the answer to any question you could ever have at your fingertips at all times.

In my example of persevering through the old, negative stories and meanings I assigned to living with diabetes, I began thinking about all of the positive things diabetes had brought into my life, and now these are my default thoughts when I think of diabetes.

Things like how deeply in touch I am with my body and all the signs it is always sending me. How intricately I understand food and exercise and the effects they have on the human body on a physiological level. How many incredible, supportive friends the diabetes community has bestowed upon me. How I am able to continually inspire others with my stories of struggles with and triumphs over the disease. How living with diabetes every single day has shaped me into an incredibly empathetic, capable, resilient human being with an uncanny ability for problem-solving and handling high levels of life-or-death related stress in a calm and collected manner.

Remember this for current challenges—you've made it through 100% of your life so far. You don't *have to* persevere, you *get to* persevere. When you change your perspective from seeing crucial aspects of your life and caring for yourself and others as chores or burdens to privileges and blessings, your experience of life will inevitably change for the better.

TAKE ACTION

List the things in your life that you get to do—things that if you didn't get to do would make an enormous difference in your overall quality of life.

Think about the perspectives in which you see these things and the priorities you assign them in your daily life, remembering that perspective always drives *practice*.

Truly consider the things you may currently be seeing from the perspective of chores or burdens, which, without the option of *getting to* do them, would greatly decrease your quality of life as you know it currently.

Practice consciously and intentionally shifting your perspective to appreciation and gratitude for the things that you get to do, like drinking clean water, eating nutrient-dense food, walking, seeing, breathing, taking insulin or any other life-sustaining medication. Without these blessings, your circumstances would ultimately suck *so much worse* than anything you are currently experiencing.

You get to do these things. They are not guaranteed. They are not promised. When you feel like you *have to* do these things, like they are burdens; that is the emotion you will equate to the experience—*you will feel burdened by your blessings.*

Don't allow yourself to feel burdened by your blessings. You can always change your perspective as many times as you want or need.

Change your emotions related to these experiences from disdain to pure gratitude so you can feel that in your heart every time you get to do them.

What amazing things do you *get to* do every day?

NEVER GIVE UP LESSON 2: FOR OTHERS

"When something is important enough, you do it even if the odds aren't in your favor."
—Elon Musk

BY BILL

Humans will often do far more for others than we will even consider doing for ourselves. We can use that to our advantage by developing a sense of purpose, a meaningful way that we look at our life that adds value to humanity and the Earth. By cultivating a higher purpose that we'll never give up on, we enable ourselves to focus on contributing more versus hoping to receive. It's a very empowering distinction.

Over a million books have been written that address finding, creating, and embracing your purpose. That's a testament to how important the topic is to our society. It's also a good indicator that there is a lot of ground to cover in that area, far more than can be covered in a single chapter. So it would be smart to plan on making purpose and meaning an ongoing, lifelong study.

This section will be a mini crash course, focusing in on the Five Ps of perseverance of which purpose is but one of them. Here they are:

- Passion
- Purpose
- Plan
- Persistence
- Persistence

There's not much you can't accomplish with passion, purpose, a plan, and lots of persistence. Read through this section and re-read it at various times in your life as your passions, purpose, and definitely your plans will change with time.

PASSION

When it comes to making sure that we don't give up on things that matter to us, it's important to align ourselves with the things we are passionate about in life. That simply means identifying the things we enjoy—that make us feel joy when talking about or participating in them—and knowing what we love to do.

We talked about this a bit in the Love Lesson section. The more we set ourselves up to do things we love to do, the more successful we will be in all areas of our lives.

Like most people, you are likely going to spend a lot of time—many, many hours—working at your job, pursuing your goals, and doing the things you define as making you feel "successful." It's a good idea to keep an eye out and use self-awareness to identify the things that actually make you *feel happy*.

Otherwise, you may get caught up working a job so that *someday* in the future you might feel happy. For us, that's a hard no. Instead, you can choose to feel happy *now* by prioritizing more of the things you're passionate about.

It's important to keep in mind that you don't have to tie everything back to a job, career, or education. In fact, it is incredibly beneficial to seek out ways to express your passion creatively through quality of life enhancements such as learning a new language or musical instrument, taking a course in writing, cooking, painting, singing, or some other form of creative expression.

Make plans to travel to new cities or countries, or try out a new restaurant or museum in your neighborhood. The point is to stop putting off what makes you happy until "later," and to intentionally prioritize engaging in experiences that align with your passions. The joy you feel from those experiences are guaranteed to carry over into other areas of your life.

At this point it would be useful to define passion as an intense desire or enthusiasm for something—for anything. This is where you truly find out who you are and what you like and begin separating from what others think—separating from what you think your parents or society expect you to like or think you "should" enjoy, which truly doesn't matter in the grand scheme of things.

When you take time to focus in on your passions and desires, you'll gain more clarity on the things that are truly important in your life, and the goals you achieve in respect to your passions will give you a deeply satisfying sense of accomplishment and fulfillment.

- This is what Napoleon Hill refers to in his success principles as a "burning desire."
- This is what Les Brown means when he says "You gotta be hungry!"
- This is what Tony Robbins is referring to when he says "Live with passion!"

This isn't to say blindly follow your passions, instead it's to say cultivate your passions, stoke the fires around them, and then take things to the next level by aligning your passion-based choices with your purpose.

Simply put: make it a top priority to do more of the things that bring you joy. Period.

PURPOSE

Let's start with a question: Why are you reading this book?

A quick definition of "why" is: for what reason or purpose.

So, for what reason or purpose are you reading this book? To improve your life in some way? To find a way to help a family member or friend? Or maybe just because it showed up in your life at the right time. The answers could be as varied as we as individuals are, which is nearly infinite.

The point is to start thinking more about why you do all the things that you do, and if you want to take these things to the next level, figure out your greater purpose(s) in life and start to organize your life around that purpose.

If you don't have a *reason* for why you're doing something, you won't get very far before giving up.

Here are some reasons that we've heard many times from clients, and have also said ourselves throughout our lives: I want to be a positive role model for my family and friends. I'm tired of being in pain and feeling down all the time and want to feel good. I want get more physically fit/strong so I can be a role model for my kids/family. I know I'm successful, but I want to feel like I'm making a positive impact on the world.

These are just a few examples of many people's "whys."

These are the juicy reasons that get us out of bed in the morning. Purpose also keeps us working late into the evening sometimes, especially if we're looking at it from an entrepreneurial standpoint. Your why is what gives you power and drive to find and act in alignment with your purpose.

If you don't know what your purpose is, that's okay. I've worked in construction, fence installation, and cutting down trees. I worked as a barista and in a car rental place. I was in the Army. I worked in cybersecurity. I worked in innovation. I continue to work as a writer, speaker, coach, and more. Daniele has been a waitress, bartender, chef, restaurant and office manager, realtor, and more, and she now works as a professional speaker, writer, coach, consultant, and so much more.

The full list of careers we've explored for both of us combined is about twenty-plus different things, and we did all these different things because, in many aspects, we were trying to explore our options and discover what got us excited. Once we were able to find out what those things were, our purposes became finding our purpose.

If you don't feel that you currently have a purpose, then let me suggest a great beginning purpose is to find your purpose. To get started, you can simply say, *"My purpose is to be a strong, kind and loving person, to improve my life, and to help others along the way."*

Those three simple statements of purpose, if acted upon, will carry you far upwards and onwards along the path as you continue to hone in on what brings you true joy.

Another great idea to consider when searching for your purpose is volunteering your time for a variety of charitable organizations that helps people and/or animals who are going through tough times since it both helps others feel better and also feels amazing to contribute to something bigger than yourself. Do what you can with what you have where you are right now.

Sometimes purpose changes over time. Your purpose might originally be to find your purpose. If you're a parent, your purpose might be loving your children, teaching them kindness, and providing them with a joyful life. If you're a college student and you're really excited about what you're learning, your purpose might be to get your degree and land the job you desire at the time, and carry on with the legacy you want to build and share with the world.

Ideally, you will work toward bringing your passion and purpose into alignment, and one of the best ways to do that is to come up with a plan.

PLAN

A plan is an intentional decision about what one is going to do. A written plan is a detailed proposal for doing or achieving something. One of the main aspects of my career has been project management, both at the professional and personal level.

You must have a plan. That plan must be written down, and you must also be willing to revise and edit it regularly along your journey. The plan is meant to list the actions that, if taken, will get you from point A to point B. The plan is simply a map showing where you are, where you want to be, and the roads you plan to take to get from here to there.

For many of us, the plan is to escape our current circumstances. If you are suffering, in pain, or struggling to overcome something horrendous in your life, you need to develop an escape plan. If you are truly ready to get to a next level in your life, that means choosing productive courses of action so that you're *doing* things rather than having things done to you—being proactive versus reactive.

Once you identify your destination, the best tool you have in getting there is to use planning that includes goal-setting, scheduling, and tracking to stay on-task. (We'll talk about those in our Take Action section.)

PERSISTENCE AND PERSISTENCE

When you put in the work of identifying your passion, purpose, and plan, you have 50% of the challenge solved. Now is when you take action!

When you take action, you'll find that doorways will be opened up for you that you couldn't have planned on or anticipated. Synchronistic connections will be made with people, the perfect piece of information will seemingly "coincidentally" fall into your lap, and you'll start to notice all the things that will help you accomplish your goals everywhere you look.

Something else will also happen. You'll run into resistance, obstacles, and challenges galore. This is where the fourth and fifth P come into play—persistence and persistence. No, that last sentence wasn't a typo. It's meant to symbolize the need to be as tenacious and as perseverant as you can be—to never give up on going after what you want.

Persistence is defined as continuing a course of action in spite of difficulty or opposition. Like I said, your purpose may change, and your plan will change. Things will come up and set you off track, but when you factor in those setbacks and course corrections and you reassess on an ongoing basis, you will be able to hone in more effectively on a life that is truly meaningful to you.

When your passion, purpose, and plan are combined with a double-dose of persistence and a lot of meaningful work, amazing things will happen.

PUTTING IT ALL TOGETHER

For me, I was passionate about solving problems and puzzles, as well as technology, innovation, and efficiency. This led me into the field of computer and network management.

Since I had my sense of identity taken from me, my purpose became wanting to help others become safer and more secure, which led me further down my career path into cybersecurity. My plan was heavily influenced by Brian Tracy in his book *Goals!* To paraphrase, Brian essentially said to focus on the skills that will take you to the top 10% in your profession. Once you do that, focus on the top 5%, and then the top 1% in roughly 5-year increments.

These various aspects led to me becoming one of the top cybersecurity professionals on the planet.

Think about some areas of life where you've already found what you define as success. Then, apply the 5 Ps and watch your progress skyrocket. It's about working smarter, then harder!

HATERS GONNA HATE

Side note: A word of caution when it comes to taking action in the areas of passion, purpose, and "your why." While there are a lot amazing reasons for discovering and creating these for yourself, there are a handful of people out in the world who thrive on putting others down for trying to better their lives.

There are a lot of reasons people do this, the main reason stemming from feeling insecure or unloving themselves. When someone does this, it is possible they have not had the success in their own life that they think they "should" have, and asserting themselves toward bringing others down to their level of defeat brings them some empty version of comfort and validation. You do not need to pay attention to this if you so choose.

Your job is not to figure out why they try to bring you down, rather, your job is to find out what works for you regarding blocking out negativity when it inevitably rears its ugly head.

That includes trying out the exercises suggested in this book, exploring other purpose-living frameworks, and ultimately deciding what works best for you. You may never come across people like this, but if you do, you'll be prepared to live your life on your own terms versus feeding into their stories and meanings.

Haters gonna hate, and players gonna play. So resolve to be a player and don't worry about what the haters say.

TAKE ACTION

Our action item for this section is to think or write in your journal about some of the things you're truly passionate about. List five specific passions completely disregarding any real or perceived blocks such as time, money, or the need for perfection. Passions are things that, when you are involved with them, you feel joyous.

Next, write down your purpose. What is your purpose in life? What is your why?

What is your plan to move forward in one area of your life, be it with your relationships, career, business, health, happiness? List three things you will do in the next year. Could one of those three things be done in the next month? The next hour?

What three things could you do that would double your level of happiness in the next six months? What three things would bring you massive happiness over the course of the next year?

Once you figure out what these things are, it's time to plan. Set a goal. Write this down: *"Within six months, I will start to perform X activity on a daily basis."*

Bring up a calendar app—or a real, paper calendar, and schedule a check-in date for that activity with a pop-up alarm and reminder. On that day, you will self-evaluate your progress toward that goal. In the meantime, follow-up on that goal, preferably on a weekly basis, to track how well you're progressing toward that goal.

If that all sounds very simplistic, that is intentional. Keep it simple!

If this sounds challenging, that's okay too! You'll get better the more you *practice*.

Don't forget to volunteer and take full advantage of the power of contribution. Look for an organization to volunteer your time with, no matter how much or little time you think you have available. www.volunteermatch.org is a great website to check out and get started.

Bill and Daniele Hargenrader | 137

NEVER GIVE UP LESSON 3: FOR THE WORLD

"**What we focus on, we empower and enlarge. Good multiplies when focused upon. Negativity multiplies when focused upon. The choice is ours: Which do we want more of?**"

—Julia Cameron

Let's massively change the world for the better, together. We're going to hold that vision once again. If the actions we've learned regarding never giving up on ourselves—by having love and forgiveness for ourselves and others, by believing that we live in a benevolent Universe by sheer example of being alive, whether you believe in God or are just grateful for the chance to exist at this time in life and on this planet—are put into action by enough people at the same time, change for the better is simply inevitable.

This is evidenced by the Maharishi Effect, or Transcendental Meditation, which has, in a variety of cases throughout history, proven that if a significant number of individuals (1% of the people in a given area) *practice* the Transcendental Meditation technique together, they can produce measurable improvements in the quality of life for the whole population.

All we are is energy. When we consciously and intentionally direct our energy towards a singular focus toward improving the quality of life for all and we do it as a group, powerful, mind-blowing things happen.

There are so many opportunities around you. You must believe in your ever-evolving purpose, finding that purpose, creating that purpose, and basing your actions on that purpose. When you never give up on the meanings you choose to make from life's experiences—that it's happening for you, not to you—then even in the most trying of circumstances, even in death, you can still be the best version of yourself. That's what it's really about.

Choose to take responsibility for the person you see in the mirror, knowing that when you grow as an individual, you also contribute to the greater good of all of humanity and the Earth itself. Start thinking about the changes that you've been hoping, wishing, and dreaming for. Write them down in your journal. Think about how to make those changes now. Write that down in your journal as well. Take action, no matter how big or small—one foot in front of the other!

Every journey starts and continues by putting one foot in front of the other. If you continue on your path with the intention of showing yourself and others that living a life filled with love, forgiveness, and perseverance is possible regardless of circumstance, you can undoubtedly rebound from whatever struggles you've gone and have yet to go through.

At any point in this process, you can start to give back, to be of service and contribute to others. Napoleon Hill said "Do not wait; the time will never be 'just right.' Start where you stand and work with whatever tools you may have at your command and better tools will be found as you go along."

This is extremely important to do in the sense of helping others. There is always someone you can help no matter where you are on your journey, and there is no better way to help yourself feel more love than to help someone else—kindness is always free to give. Help others grow, and in doing so, you will also help yourself grow; it is always a win-win situation. This is how we can make a massive change on a global scale.

TAKE ACTION

Your action item—which you may know by now—is to paint a beautiful picture in your mind of a positive future for our world.

Write it in your journal, say it aloud, or at a minimum take a few moments to contemplate. Take some time to think about what the world would look and feel like if everyone on this planet *never gave up* on being the best person they could be and helping others along the way. We will all stumble, we will all falter, we will all make mistakes, but what if we all never give up? What if we continue to work towards the highest good for all?

Working toward your destiny is about taking action to move you away from pain and suffering much more often and toward a world of more joy, enthusiasm, and believing that it is possible to be a better person tomorrow than we are today, every day, no matter what.

That's how the world changes. It changes when *you* change—everything and everyone is connected.

Always remember that "we" starts with "me."

Paint the picture of a world where everybody never gives up on being their best self. Where everybody loves more, where everybody forgives more. What kind of world would that feel like to live in? Then, start living it. Start *being* it so others can see it.

YOUR LIVING LEGACY AND FACING DEATH

"At the end of our lives, we all ask did I live? Did I love? Did I matter?"
—Brendon Burchard

Our section on never giving up wouldn't be complete without addressing your living legacy. Your living legacy is the ripples of your thoughts, intentions, actions, and interactions as felt and remembered by those you come into contact with throughout your life and also in death.

Whether we're ready for it or not, death has many powerful lessons to teach, and we all have to learn them one way or another. No one lives forever. There is, after all, an undeniable circle of life, and death is a part of that circle.

We wrote this heartfelt book on loving more, bettering your life, and striving to achieve worthwhile goals, and since death is an unavoidable part of life, we wanted to address it in the context of the intentions of this book.

Maybe you haven't had to deal with death directly in your own life yet, *or* perhaps you've gone through the experience of losing friends, family members, or someone very close to you.

Maybe you yourself are facing the possibility or reality of death due to illness or other circumstances beyond your control, or are choosing to be there to comfort someone else who is facing death in this more immediate manner.

Or maybe you are someone who, while reading this book, is caught up in the maelstrom of considering taking your own life like too many others who chose suicide as the best option based on the tools available to them at the time and the circumstances they were experiencing.

In any of these cases, if you need help, *please, please, please* reach out and ask for it. It's available to you by way of books, support groups, blogs, online forums, hotlines, and more that are just a Google search away. And if your situation is dire, you can go to the Suicide Prevention Lifeline's website at suicidepreventionlifeline.org to get immediate support.

Our intention is not to address all aspects of the death, dying, and grieving process, but to focus on the areas that apply to living a life filled with conscious and intentional meaning *right now*—from wherever you stand now until this current iteration of your life is called to an end.

While writing this book, we interviewed and learned from some extraordinary people. And we had the sad and inspiring experience of learning lessons about death from one of the most kind and caring people that we've ever known.

My cousin Lisa was a joyful, kind, beautiful mother, wife, daughter, and friend to many. She was full of energy, had a zest for living life in the moment, was a caring nurse, and exemplified living a life full of love, being forgiving, and never giving up.

In her last year of life at the age of 40, Lisa had the challenge of figuring out how to battle advanced cancer and still live a fulfilled life. This would be devastating for anybody. But what is so powerful is the role model she became for our family and her friends. She approached death in such a beautiful, proactive way.

She did not want anyone to feel sorry for her because she had cancer. She wanted to live happily until she died. She cherished her relationships with her family and friends. When her doctor walked into Lisa's room to give her negative news about her diagnosis, he would somehow walk out of the room feeling better than when he walked in—she just had a way about her that made people feel good.

It certainly wasn't easy, and I know it was far more painful for her family closest to her, but when we had our family gatherings during this time of transition, it wasn't about being sad and somber. It was about celebrating life. She did not give up—she stood up to cancer.

Shortly after she passed, we attended her celebration of life ceremony on the Avalon beach with her mother (my aunt Judy who remained so strong and loving throughout)—and we watched Ken, Rob, and Robert (Lisa's husband, step-father, and brother) take her ashes out into the ocean where she always loved to be, especially with her young daughter Amelia—it was an incredibly moving experience.

The way that Lisa held herself and comforted her daughter while family, friends, and coworkers came together throughout the experience was a powerful example of how to live and a legacy that will be remembered and treasured. It brings tears to my eyes to write about it—tears of sadness and tears of love and gratitude.

Here are some words that Judy so graciously shared with us:

When living with a terminal disease of your child, I found my daughter Lisa simply needed my authentic love. After diagnosis, during her illness, and now that she is gone, Lisa did not want people to feel sorry for her, or her husband, or her child. She lived a life of dignity then and does so now in her death.

The death of my child reminded me of the importance of time and living in the present moment. As Lisa said, she was so grateful for our families' love and constant support, it really made her learn the importance of life.

In my daughter's death, I am finding peace in that love is stronger than death. Life is all about the quality of life we live, the love we share together, and the lasting memories we make.

LIVING A LIFE ON PURPOSE

Discussing death can be a challenging subject because we have spent so much time talking about how we can move forward, find our purpose, and persevere against all odds. Sometimes, bad things happen, and no human alive can escape that reality. It's how we respond to those things that determines our quality of life in every minute, every day.

We might have a goal, make a plan and put it into action, and even with the best laid plans we might not reach that goal. But that doesn't mean that we're not worthy or that the goal was foolish. It doesn't mean we didn't persevere. It just means it didn't happen this time with this plan.

When we set up our life up to be *on purpose*—to have passion, purpose, and a plan to pursue those things and keep moving forward—the setbacks are simply part of the journey for everyone.

When we set our purpose to be the best person that we can be—the best son or daughter, best husband or wife, best father or mother, to inspire people and inspire ourselves—if we live this way while keeping the inevitability of an end in mind, then if tragedy strikes, we are more readily able to face what comes.

This is how we create a legacy. A legacy is something that is passed on to others—wisdom, character, and values that affect those around us. We don't have to be famous in any way at all to leave a legacy. We all leave one.

It's what people think of when they remember you, how people feel when they think about you. It's something—*a feeling*— that you leave behind when you pass on.

As Maya Angelou so wisely said, "People will forget what you said, people will forget what you did, but *people will never forget how you made them feel*."

When you focus on living a life that not only helps yourself but also intentionally helps others, you are creating a living legacy that goes far beyond yourself.

When you express your love, forgiveness, and perseverance through spoken or written words and actions, others have no choice but to see and feel that and, more often than not, they want to do something similar themselves.

There's a great passage from Felix Adler, founder of the Ethical Culture Movement, that sums up the powerful lesson death teaches us:

The bitter, yet merciful, lesson which death teaches us is to distinguish the gold from the tinsel, the true values from the worthless chaff. The terrible events of life are great eye-openers. They force us to learn that which it is wholesome for us to know, but which habitually we try to ignore—namely, that really we have no claim on a long life; that we are each of us liable to be called off at any moment, and that the main point is not how long we live, but with what meaning we fill the short allotted span...

CELEBRATING LIFE

If you're reading this, then you are alive. The fact that you are alive is nothing short of a miracle when we look at the vastness of the Universe and our place in it.

That alone is a cause for celebration!

Some of us have been taught that celebration is a bad thing, or that we should only do it on special occasions like a birthday, holiday, or when a sports team wins the big game.

In order to make feeling good a priority, we need to celebrate life; not just our birthdays, but every day. We do that by expressing gratitude and allowing ourselves to feel joy and by helping others that have gone through similar struggles. We do this by saying *thank you* for the opportunity to experience life.

We must truly love ourselves—consistently give ourselves credit and kudos for all we have accomplished, big and small— and celebrate every single win, no matter how insignificant we might perceive it to be.

Nothing is too small to be celebrated. *Nothing.* If we don't love who we are *now* and feel pride in our character as a human being, we will never fully commit to change because we won't truly feel deserving of the happiness that comes along with achieving our goals.

And if we don't feel we are deserving of happiness and all of the joys that life has to offer, then no amount of effort or motivation will ever be sustained for very long.

TAKE ACTION

The action item and journal entry for the day is to think of someone that has passed on, a family member or pet perhaps, and journal or take time out to meditate on and think about the lessons you're grateful to have learned from them that they have passed on to you.

Take it one step further and think about your living legacy. What are the messages and impressions you currently bring to the world and what impact are your efforts having on those around you? How do you want to make others feel?

Start to live, to choose your actions, as if those messages and impacts are already there, even if you don't feel they are quite yet. If they're not, think about some ways you can change your actions so the impact you have on others is what you desire it to be.

The next action item is creating your life celebration *practice*. Write out the words on a sheet of paper or Post-it Note: *Thank You. Thank You. Thank You.*

Then put that paper where you'll see it in the morning, noon, and night, and say the words upon waking, once during the day, and once before bed. Say them with feeling, heart, soul, and commitment to celebrating the amazing opportunity of getting to be alive.

HERO'S QUEST: NEVER GIVE UP!

"Then let us be rid of it, once and for all. Come, Mr. Frodo! I can't carry it for you, but I can carry you. Come on!"
—Sam Gamgee, *The Lord of the Rings* by J.R.R. Tolkien

You fought hard, pushed yourself beyond your limits, faced death, and forged a stronger sense of self.

And now you have earned the Sword of Perseverance!

You hold the sword in your hand and hold the flat of the blade up to your face where you see your reflection—you see your true self, emboldened by your passion, purpose, plan, and will to never give up!

You are the hero of your story. While we have to be open to accepting help, we also have to realize that we are the only ones who can save ourselves.

You always have your protective Shield of Love strapped to your back, your healing Orb of Forgiveness in your satchel, and, sheathed at your hip, your powerful Sword of Perseverance.

The magical nature of these artifacts of power allows for them to be worn without being seen. Right now, you can feel them upon your person and feel empowered by their presence.

You realize now that you've always had these gifts at your side… Now you know how to use them. You must *practice* with them, become proficient, and wield them to their utmost ability so that you can reach your highest level.

You now stand ready to face your demons, slay your dragons, collect your treasure, save the day, and help others along the way.

But your quest is really just beginning…

You're running with the big dogs now, you're no longer a pup.

Gather your courage and keep moving 'cause it's time to:

LEVEL UP!

YOUR STORY PART 6: LEVEL UP!

"The path to success is to take massive, determined action."
—Anthony Robbins

All right... Here we go!

You've learned lots of new valuable skills, put deep thought in to your personal hero's journey, taken action in areas that mean the most to you, and gained experience in progressing in your hero's journey. Now it's time to level up!

You're going to integrate all the areas you learned so far and take your mastery to a new level.

You're almost to the finish line. Time to ramp it up as you're crossing into the third act, moving towards the final showdown and climax of the book.

This is where Luke and the rebels make their Death Star bombing run on a small thermal exhaust port.

This is where Simba returns home to confront Scar amidst the flames of Pride Rock.

This is where Frodo and Sam make their final push up the face of Mt. Doom to destroy the ring once and for all.

This is where *you* confront whatever is holding you back face to face... and emerge victorious!

Our intention with this book is to include our most powerful stories *and the critical lessons we've learned through living those stories*. Our aim is to guide you on your path to a life that feels whole and connected so you can make progress in whatever ways you choose.

One of our biggest challenges we had was keeping this book short enough that it could be read in one sitting if chosen, powerful enough so it could be impactful immediately, and have enough depth so that it could be re-read time and time again.

What this means is there are a lot of content, lessons, tips, and strategies that we would have liked to include, as well as topics that we would love to expound on that will have be saved for future books in the series.

For now, though, this is the start of the final section of this book... And we're giving it all we've got!

In this section we share with you how to effectively combine the *practices* of love, forgiveness, and never giving up in your daily life for lasting success.

We're going to answer the promise in the book of giving you a plan of action to implement love, forgiveness, and never giving up daily in your life, and we will include some important areas we know will be helpful for you on your journey of learning more about your infinitely powerful connection to yourself and the rest of the world.

This is your story. This is your life—your Next Level Life. Let's do this!

TURN ADVERSITY INTO ADVANTAGE

*"Every adversity, every failure, every heartache carries
with it the seed of an equal or greater benefit."*
—Napoleon Hill

BY DANIELE

By now you may have begun to realize—through the vehicles of
our collective stories as well as your own self-reflection and
personal experience—how any adversity can be turned to an
advantage through love, forgiveness, and perseverance.

We're going to summarize a couple of examples and
encourage you to think about any and all prior perceived
adversity or limitation in your own life and how you can use it
to your advantage and to the advantage of others.

For me, type 1 diabetes was a perceived adversity and
weakness for almost fifteen years. Living with a chronic disease
has now become one of the most meaningful and profound
strengths and advantages of my life. Diabetes has allowed me to
find my once-buried passion for human wellness, both my own
and others—mind, body, and spirit. I am in touch with my
inner wisdom in ways that ten years ago I would have said were
voodoo—the way I manifest "coincidences" and synchronicities
has become the everyday norm in our lives.

Through cultivating a strong mindset and healthy habits in
order to persevere through adversity, I am now an expert
researcher, experimenter, and citizen scientist and believe that I
am healthier (including all blood work markers) than the
majority of people my age who do not have a chronic disease
because I have a chronic disease. Outward of my physical health, the
friendships and connections I've gained from the empathetic
badasses that make up the diabetes community are profound.
The people I've been privileged to help reach new heights
throughout their own wellness journeys are extraordinarily
fulfilling.

It does us good to look around and seek out how our
friends and family have faced adversity and succeeded despite

or because of the odds. In our case, Bill and I have a good friend named Alex who was born with athetoid cerebral palsy and has one of the most astounding and ongoing adversity to advantage stories fueled by his own will to never give up and his desire to help others. He's visited over 35 countries and 150 cities independently (read: alone) with his power wheelchair in tow.

He's been skydiving, on an African safari, and has dealt with levels of discrimination that most of us cannot even fathom. His experiences and insights have led to him starting his own businesses and training and presenting to some of the biggest companies in the world on equality and inclusiveness.

Alex is the inventor of the Freedom One Wheelchair. Travelling worldwide in his power wheelchair meant constant and never-ending breakdowns, as his wheelchair was not designed to last a full day for an active adult.

Alex continually had his freedom ripped from him in seconds, all because his chair couldn't keep up with him. This gave him significant first-hand experience of the limitations that are imposed upon people by power wheelchairs, which are outdated and prohibitively expensive.

His vision of an improved power wheelchair product and service started from knowing that the product absolutely had to change and has now grown into a funded and developing business with support and backing from both public and private sectors in the UK, as well as a functional prototype. Now advancing through adversity is leading to an advantage for Alex and so many others.

RIPPLES THROUGH TIME

Throughout history we can turn to so many examples of humans turning adversity into advantage no matter what the circumstances presented. Harriet Tubman is an extraordinary inspiration in this realm. From being born into slavery, escaping, and subsequently making some thirteen missions to rescue approximately seventy enslaved people, to becoming the first woman to lead an armed expedition in the Civil War freeing more than 700 slaves.

She is truly a historical icon of courage, love, forgiveness, never giving up, and paying it forward to the greater good of humanity. When we look for it, we can see the echoes of Harriet's bravery and advancement in the face of adversity reflected in our daily lives in the present.

In modern times, Oprah Winfrey is one of our favorite examples of the ability to turn adversity into advantage—all the while focusing on love, forgiveness, and never giving up. Her childhood included repeated accounts of sexual abuse, rape, and severe physical beatings. She was sent to a juvenile detention home at 13, and at 14 gave birth to a premature baby that died soon after.

None of these unfortunate and tragic experiences stopped her from becoming the first black anchor on Nashville's TV news station, hosting a number-one ranked talk show for fourteen seasons, winning 34 Emmys, initiating the National Child Protection Act that eventually got signed into law establishing the first national database of convicted child abusers, and becoming one of the most influential people of the 20th century in the ways of love, forgiveness, and perseverance.

Lessons on harnessing adversity as a force for growth are contained in the stories told of legends of old to our modern-day leaders that have pushed through their prior limits. From feats of greatness you witnessed from friends and family to times in your own personal experience where you've stepped it up and pulled through when times were tough.

The clues are all around us if we just learn to look for them. The master key to success in dealing with adversity is captured in the opening quote by Napoleon Hill. Learn to *always* look for a seed of greater or equivalent benefit in the challenges you meet, and you will begin to transform yourself to higher levels of greatness.

The positive effects of doing so can be seen when we look at humanity from a historical perspective. We see how acts of courage and faith in the past have opened the doors for us in the present to become more of our best selves.

Now you must walk through those doors that others have already opened and work on opening the doors that you have been uniquely called to open yourself.

Since *you are the only you that will ever exist*, nobody can ever do what you are meant to do in the way you are meant to do it with the keys that you already have and can continue to hone in on through pushing through and leveraging adversity.

TAKE ACTION

Take a moment now to journal or reflect: Do you have any examples in your own life where you can see how someone, maybe even yourself, turned adversity into an advantage?

What are some challenges currently in your life that you can see as an opportunity to grow?

TURN TRAGEDY INTRO TRIUMPH

"Although there may be tragedy in your life, there's always a possibility to triumph. It doesn't matter who you are, where you come from. The ability to triumph begins with you. Always."
—Oprah Winfrey

BY BILL

So how do you turn tragedy into triumph? It's helpful to look at the definitions.

Tragedy is an event or circumstance that causes great suffering, destruction, and distress, such as a serious accident, crime, or natural catastrophe, whereas the definition of triumph is to achieve a victory and be successful in an effort.

So when we say turn tragedy into triumph, what we're really saying is to seek out the way to transform a painful event into a successful outcome in some way, shape, or form.

Right from the start we know that there will be tragic events that occur in life no matter what. Pain and suffering are a part of life, but by realizing that we can use that pain to propel us forward instead of only viewing it as an anchor weighing us down, we can start to look at life from a whole new perspective and stop suffering so much.

Like a bow and arrow, the more the drawstring is pulled back, the more the tension increases to drive it forward. And when the command is given to release the string, the arrow shoots forward—much, much further than where it started—travelling amazing distances at incredible speeds to its intended target!

You are that arrow. A tragedy in your life can feel like you are being pulled backward, but when you realize that we all have within us the ability to use that which is holding us back to actually propel us forward, that's when we learn that our darkest moments can be the sources of our greatest strength.

In my personal example of being an 8-year-old boy locked away in a mental institution for a crime I didn't commit, I felt intense suffering and pain as my trust in family, doctors, police, God, and even myself was warped and twisted. But through that tragic experience, that deep level of suffering revealed strength of character that I would not have otherwise experienced for a long time—or maybe not at all.

In essence, I had to grow up very quickly to survive. I had to learn to become my own mentor, my own guide, and this ingrained in me a fierce drive and resiliency that I still use to this day.

One might make the point that an 8-year-old boy shouldn't have to lose his innocence and fend for himself in that way, and to them I would say that I didn't have a choice. Or rather, my choice was to never give up on figuring out a way out of that nightmare or give in to the years of despair.

No matter what age you are, that's always the choice you have when confronted with a tragedy. Even when things seem most bleak and you feel weaker than you ever have before, you still can make the choice to salvage all that is good inside of you, *fully knowing* that there is a better tomorrow.

It took me 2 years in the mental institution to realize the power and lessons of love. It took me another 10 years to realize the true power of forgiveness, but even then, I still carried wounds and felt the darkness inside of me from the events that had befallen me. And it would take another 10 years before I was able to look back and see the powerful lesson of perseverance that shaped my destiny when I realized that my darkest moment, my first night in the padded cell, led to my greatest strength.

That greatest strength isn't in how strong I am, it's how I can help others become stronger individuals by sharing my experiences vulnerably and honestly. It's how I take my horrible situation and tell others the lessons I learned, and if you listen and apply the lessons, my genuine hope is that it won't take you two decades of life to conquer your demons, face your fears, and step into your greatness.

You already possess the ability to attain that kind of strength for yourself and help others along the way—you always have and you always will.

A BETTER PATH

The funny thing is you never know when a tragedy will steer you in a different direction than your originally set course; it could actually take you to a much better and more desirable destination.

Take for instance the personal journey of my friend, Qigong teacher and healer, David Beaudry. Like many of us, David played sports in high school. He went on to continue to play football at the college level until a devastating knee injury sidelined him. So much of his identity, passion, time, and effort that had gone into playing football, into being an athlete, was shattered in an instant.

Through the shadow of depression, David persevered and searched for the deeper meaning in this event. This led David down the path to attaining a psychology degree, traveling the world, training, *practicing*, and attaining a master's in Medical Qigong, focusing on health, wellness, and energy cultivation.

Through finding a way to heal his own injuries—mind, body, and spirit—on a deeper level, David unlocked his gifts as a healer that gave him a new perspective on what true fitness means to him. He now instructs others on their path to better living whether from a computer screen, in a massive crowd at a seminar, or barefoot, breathing in cool crisp mountain air in a personalized workshop. What was once perceived as a tragedy led to a massive triumph for himself and everyone David inspires, myself included!

And who can forget how Bruce Wayne turned tragedy into triumph as he turned the pain of losing his parents in an armed robbery as he watched helplessly into a life of fighting crime and saving Gotham and the world on more than one occasion as the caped crusader known as Batman.

What, you thought the people you look up to and admire have to be real? Not at all. Art imitates life, and life imitates art in an ongoing cycle where the best of humanity (and worst) can be exemplified on the page and screen. So take your pick of heroes and heroines to add to your personal team from Harry Potter to Hermione Granger, Spider-man to Wonder Woman, Luke Skywalker to Rey, and beyond.

Now we're not suggesting you dress up as a bat and fight crime, but it never hurts to have a magic wand or a cape on hand. Just saying.

BLAZE YOUR TRAIL TO TRIUMPH

By keeping an open mind and having faith that you will figure it out, you are shifting your focus from the pain of the perceived problem and realigning it with hope and possibility.

People often try to get out of a hole by digging it deeper. In reality, they need to put down the shovel and start making some rope and every now and then giving a shout for help and reading books and following examples of how others got out of holes like the one they are in.

Here are some "benefits" of tragedy to keep in mind:

- Tragedy gives you an external force that can drive you through suffering, and that suffering can lead you to find answers you may not have otherwise discovered.
- Tragedy can force you to seek better mentors and become your own mentor.
- Tragedy shakes things up and forces you to take action now, especially in areas you've been wanting to change for a long time.

The following are some motivators to keep in mind that will help guide you in blazing your trail to triumph:

- Dedicate your success to a loved one that passed on or is still alive that helped you in some way, by example or through direct action.
- Focus on recovering, healing, embracing your wholeness, and feeling better so that you can help others in a similar situation.
- Drive yourself to get through the tragic situation so that you can set a positive example for your family, friends, and community.

While a tragedy can have a lasting effect, in order to turn it into a triumph, we need to look at that tragedy as a temporary event. And while your success might not come overnight, with time and conditioning we can learn to assign new meanings to any pain and suffering that transforms it into motivation and momentum much sooner.

TAKE ACTION

Take a moment now to reflect: Do you have any experiences in your own life you can look back on that felt tragic at the time, but eventually led to something good or even great? What are some ways you can continue to grow stronger now and into the future?

WHAT ABOUT ME?

"No one is useless in this world who lightens the burdens of another."
— Charles Dickens

Sometimes people see these stories of others overcoming the odds and they get sad they don't have a huge tragedy to overcome. They may feel like something is missing in their life, or they expected more from themselves—they see people that have had less resources than they have making their way in the world and they shut down.

First off, congrats! While we have gone through diabetes (and will continue to love, forgive, and persevere through it until there is a cure, possibly for the rest of our lives) and wrongful imprisonment and have emerged stronger for it, Daniele would take a real cure for diabetes in a second (meaning fully functioning beta cells that are not killed off by an autoimmune response in the body without the need for immunosuppressant drugs), and I have no intention of returning to the mental institution.

That's what all this love, forgiveness, and perseverance is all about—living a life that is filled with as much joy and peace as possible.

That being said, it's understandable that someone without a major challenge in life to overcome could feel disheartened. In fact, several people we know very well have voiced this exact feeling to us, as they feel they have not gone through anything that felt massively challenging to them—and that in and of itself becomes the challenge to overcome.

Use your feelings of discontent to motivate yourself! Looking back at the definition of tragedy, it's a painful experience, and as we have been told, it can also be quite painful to not have a tragic story to recount and use to propel you forward. That in itself has proven to be painful for many. Use that challenge to drive you. You don't need a tragedy by definition to make more out of whatever it is you already have and help others do the same.

We recommend looking for other areas that you may not immediately think of that are undoubtedly challenging adversities to overcome.

Unhealthy addiction for instance, whether to drugs, alcohol, food, or anything else that keeps you feeling stuck, numb, and possibly hurts yourself and others can be used as a focal point.

Boredom, behavioral-based depression, escapism, disconnection, and general unhappiness in our lives can serve as areas to focus on because these feelings are the byproducts of a life that isn't self-guided, present, conscious, loving, forgiving, and aware—a life that isn't focused on a higher purpose.

Or you can focus on others that need help in an area that you have expertise. The options are endless.

The point is your reason for moving forward doesn't have to be a massive, headline grabbing, Earth shattering event to be immensely meaningful to yourself and others.

What it really comes down to (whether we have faced a massive tragedy, adversity, or none of the above) is that it's about the meaning we make from whatever life offers. It's about seeing others' struggles and learning from them and learning not to take what we have for granted.

It's about consciously and intentionally focusing consistently on what we do have versus what we don't have, what we can control versus what we can't control, and on remaining in the present versus in the past or in the future. Here's where our gratitude *practices* from earlier lessons really come into play.

The fact is that when nature or chance or God puts a challenge in front of us, we can always choose to see that as an opportunity to reflect and make new choices, and it gives us something new to strive for.

If we don't evolve to set our own challenges for ourselves and are just waiting for something to happen to us, this means that we're taking a passive role in our own lives—we're choosing to sit in the passenger seat when we are the only ones who can drive. We're not taking charge of our decisions and therefore actively shaping our destiny.

And while an adversity or a challenge can focus our energy, we still absolutely need to learn to focus our own energy wherever we want it to go, otherwise we can identify too much with the circumstance or challenge we face.

Remember the example of the bow and arrow we gave earlier where when life pulls you back, you can use that tension to move yourself forward? The next step in evolving your inner strength is to become aware that you aren't just the arrow, you are actually the arrow, bow, and archer all in one—very Zen, we know! It's up to you to take aim and fire at the targets (goals) you have set for yourself.

So stand strong, take aim, and fire away!

TAKE YOUR LIFE TO THE NEXT LEVEL

"Behold I do not give lectures or a little charity, when I give I give myself."
— Walt Whitman

In many ways, what we are talking about regarding striving to take our lives to the next level is actively engaging in the process and *practice* of self-actualization—the realization and fulfillment of one's talents and potentials, especially considered as a drive or need present in all living things.

Self-actualization is an ongoing effort to realize our fullest potentials in life, which is an open-ended endeavor since the potential that every human being possesses is infinite and immeasurable.

When it comes to achieving their full potential, most people have barely begun to scratch the surface. The potential in you is part of a cosmic potentiality that exists in every particle of the Universe. It exists as a field of states of what is possible in the world as we know it and it is as real as gravity.

Potentiality, however, is even more hidden from view than gravity because it exists at the mind level, and science will likely never be able to measure it with instruments or take photos of its landscape.

This includes being able to share and express your innate creativity, pursue happiness and knowledge, grow as an individual physically, mentally, and spiritually, and give back to society—to be of service to the greater good in a positive way, transforming it and yourself through your actions as so many that have come before us have demonstrated is possible.

While there are many considerations that go into motivation and the drive to realize our inherent potential, Maslow's hierarchy of needs does provide a good reference model for us to consider:

Included in the hierarchy are:
- Physiological (air, food, water, shelter, sleep)
- Safety (physical, economic)
- Love and belonging/connection (friends, intimacy, family)
- Esteem (status/ego needs, respect from others)
- Self-actualization (realizing one's fullest potential)
- Self-transcendence (considering one's self in relation to nature and the cosmos)

At what level of Maslow's above hierarchy are you spending the majority of your time, thoughts, and efforts? The case can be made that we need to spend our efforts in each of these areas to feel fulfilled and have a meaningful life; however, that decision will vary from person to person and can ultimately only be made by each of us as individuals.

This can get confusing and overwhelming quickly, so to make it easier to set goals and track progress, you can frame your efforts in the following more commonly used terminology areas, which is how Daniele and I do it: Health, Self-Development, Relationships, Wealth, and Spiritual Growth.

We recommend choosing to focus on one area to improve on at a time based on what is most important to you in your life right now (remember, not what is important to your parents, children, spouse, or anyone else—what is important *to you*) and keep the other areas in mind, or in a journal, or Google document so you can keep track of your thoughts, ideas, and desires.

If you don't take the time to prioritize what is most important to you, you will likely continue spending your valuable time and effort working on things you don't really care about and/or don't bring you joy. Take the time to list *your* priorities using joy as your internal guide.

Your deepest desires are cosmically intuitive clues to what destiny and what purpose you are here to fulfill, no matter how grand or out of reach they may seem. The choice of where to place your focus is always yours, and it is okay to change focus when you feel called to do so.

An important self-sabotage trap to avoid is looking at the body of work of others who are leaders in their field doing what you aspire to do and comparing yourself to them harshly and judgmentally. As Theodore Roosevelt said "Comparison is the thief of joy."

It's smart to learn from others who are in a place you aspire to be, but it is massively counter-productive to judge yourself negatively based on someone else's circumstances and doing so will undoubtedly hold you back from taking action. This is always true regardless of the subject matter.

No matter what area you choose to focus on, improving in any one area undoubtedly spills over into all others. You can use any area of improvement as a foothold to help build the other areas up. When you act as a leader and lead yourself consistently in the direction of progress, you can't help but to begin to sow the seeds of leadership for others who you interact with.

To live a Next Level Life is to live a purposeful life where the focus is on love, forgiveness, perseverance, progress, growth, exploration, education, collaboration, ideation, and testing things out to see what works as you are moving forward, all the while being grateful for the good things you have in your life right this very moment.

TAKE ACTION

You've likely been through a number of challenges in life no matter what age you are, and you may have developed your own story or pattern regarding how you handle successes and failures.

Contemplate and write out in your journal some of your own personal rules for success. What specifically has to happen for you to be successful in your own mind within the areas of personal development, health, wealth, and spirituality? Don't know them off hand? That's okay, most of us don't and never will until we give ourselves the gift of defining the terms of our own lives.

Take time to reflect. In your journal come up with three clearly definable benchmarks you will be able to reach in the next year that will help take your life to your next level and that will allow you to feel successful on your own terms.

LOVE, FORGIVE, NEVER GIVE UP: COMBO!

"Stop comparing your journey to anyone else's. What you came to do, be, and have is unique to you."
— Preston Smiles

Love, forgiveness, and never giving up. These are all incredibly meaningful concepts, *practices*, and feelings on their own, but the real power lies in combining them. That's the real secret to amplifying our power to turn adversity into advantage, tragedy into triumph, and take our lives to the next level.

When you combine love, forgiveness, and the will to never give up, it's like shining the sun's rays through a magnifying glass. You are essentially concentrating the energy of love to enter and fuel the areas of forgiveness and perseverance into a single point of focused energy. This is exactly what we need as a human race right now at this point in history. The world needs as much love as it can get.

It's very important to understand why we put them in the order of love, forgive, and never give up. Love comes first. If you chose just one focus of learning to love yourself more then using the fuel of that self-love to show yourself and others more kindness and understanding would unquestionably make your world a better place.

Forgiveness comes second because no matter how conscious a mindset you may have, that doesn't mean that other people we interact with will have that same mindset. As much as we both put our faith in people being inherently good, we are also very well aware that people can be mean, do harm, and attempt to force you into spending your time, thoughts, energy, and emotions on them, whether consciously or unconsciously, in effect letting them win and have your power even when they're not around by giving them your focus.

Oftentimes this usurping of energy goes on for years or even a lifetime if forgiveness fueled by love is not explored. When you enter these situations in the mindset of love first, you are much more easily able to navigate through forgiving and separating from toxic people and situations, and are more willing to accept that forgiveness is the right path to take the best care of your mind, body, and spirit wellness that you can.

Forgiveness lets you focus on you—on the self-love and self-care you need and deserve to move forward—all the while remembering that forgiveness is not forgetting, but a means of growing wiser.

So now you're choosing to act from a mindset of love, forgiving purposefully *for yourself* so you can spend your energy on your intentions and aspirations, and what you realize is that you've already been never giving up on yourself the whole time!

By focusing in on perseverance, higher purpose and connection with the foundations of love and forgiveness supporting you, you're naturally accelerating your progress towards whatever you may be working toward in a directly proportional manner.

Sometimes you won't have the luxury of choosing what order love, forgiveness, and never giving up occur, and sometimes perseverance is the only reason you're still standing after having fallen down so many times. We get that.

We simply want to be clear that it's counterproductive to aim to never give up on anything that is not fueled by love. Many people choose to hold on tight to the pain of past struggles because they believe persevering through that pain and struggle is the only reason they have accomplished anything in their lives.

Pain and struggle are temporary boosters. The further in the past any feelings of pain or struggle initiated, the weaker and weaker a source of perseverance it becomes. Eventually you must turn that pain into forgiveness or you are guaranteed to hit the ceiling of what fuel the pain or perseverance has allowed you to accomplish and remain stuck, and oftentimes you will be dragged backwards.

We can all take a lesson from nature. Nature loves, forgives, and never gives up all day, every day, always. Through billions of years, cosmic calamities and human-induced damage, Mother Earth still provides us with the love of hydration and nourishment, materials to clothe and house ourselves, and so much more.

She keeps loving us, forgiving us, and never gives up hope that we will massively increase our efforts towards healing Her and earning Her forgiveness through changing our actions. "We" starts with "me." When we heal ourselves, we heal the Earth.

DANIELE'S NEXT LEVEL LIFE STORY

"Your work is to discover your world and then with all your heart give yourself to it."
— Buddha

I'm thirty-five years old as I sit here typing these words, and I feel happier and healthier now than I ever have before in my entire life. I am healthier in mind, body, and spirit—none of which are separated in any way and are all one and the same. Further, I believe without any doubt that my experience of life will only keep getting better as long as I continue to love, forgive, and persevere.

On top of that, I am absolutely certain that no matter what challenges life places in my path, no matter how long I may stray from love, forgiveness, and perseverance, eventually I will return home. Those values, those *practices*, are my home now. This is who I am. This is my truest self.

I don't live in a fantasy world where negativity and pain don't exist. I simply do not accept them as long-term residents in my life. They are like drifters that come and go but aren't welcome to stay very long. If I feel they are overstaying their welcome, I take specific, directed actions to kick them to the curb. These actions are always based in self-love and forgiveness.

I decide how I need to care for myself in order to process negative emotions—whether I need to grieve, wallow, fall apart and come back together, get professional help, seek out peer support, forgive, accept, or any number of other actions—in order to move on. I am fully aware that negative emotions will show up again and that it has been and always will be up to me to decide how to care for myself in order to hold them at bay.

Health, joy, gratitude, love, and oneness with the Universe are my home now. I can say without any reservations that this home is much warmer and more welcoming than the angry, fearful, frustrated, hopeless, helpless home full of shame, guilt, self-pity, and self-loathing where I used to live. The only difference is that one home was built and conditioned unconsciously, and I even defended its structure for many years.

I built this new home while present, conscious, awake, and aware, and I will continue to fortify its foundations with my *practices* for as long as I shall live. This home is filled with my carefully chosen intentions for my own life.

Now that I have consciously and intentionally moved out of that old house and built this new one, one that I crafted thoughtfully with love, forgiveness, and full acceptance of my completeness, I can only envision this proverbial house getting increasingly bigger, allowing infinite room for others like you to move in and "live" in this incredibly vulnerable yet incredibly safe and truthful space with me (and Bill—he lives here, too!).

The house has infinite potential for growth into a village, a community, and there is no limit to how big this community can get. There is always enough room for anyone and everyone. You are always welcome here.

Your truth is your own. Your stories, the meanings you assign to everything you experience, and your beliefs are your own as well. They are yours to mold and shape into whatever makes you feel joy, gratitude, love, and fulfillment, or with the same amount of effort, anger, fear, guilt, shame, self-pity, and resentment.

The only difference is what you choose to focus on, the actions you choose to take, the *practices* you choose to engage in every day, and the meanings you assign to every experience you ever have in life.

What will you choose?

BILL'S NEXT LEVEL LIFE STORY

I am 38 years old, and right now, I'm looking at a picture of myself as an 8-year-old boy. In that picture, the younger version of me named Billy is looking back at me. Those were dark times, but there is a hint of hope in those eyes.

This picture, to me, feels like it captured a conduit to the past to my soul. When I look at the picture of myself, the thoughts I have are, *I'm coming. I am coming to save you.*

I want to go back and tell that boy named Billy that it's going to be okay, that we're going to get through this. That it will be tough and scary and dark, but there will be love and friendship and experience and strength. That he needs to hold on, endure, and strive to make the most meaning of his situation.

And you know what? My younger self was doing that already.

Somehow, someway, I was guided to that path, and though there were times of doubt, times when I behaved in ways that were not in line with my values, times when I lied, and times when I was self-serving, it always felt like this path was there for me.

Maybe you can feel that, too? Do you have a sense that all of this is happening for a reason? For a greater purpose?

And if we just keep walking and searching for the most positive meaning in all of this, it will work out.

I had envisioned myself at that age as the heroes in the stories I read and the adventures I watched—fighting alongside Duke and Snake Eyes on the *G.I. Joe* cartoon series or using the Force like Luke with my action figures in the backyard.

I had always envisioned myself as the hero in make-believe, and eventually, I realized the massive power in envisioning myself as a hero in my own story.

We get to decide: Are we the victim or are we the eventual victor?

But at the time the picture of Billy was taken, those connections hadn't been made yet.

Looking back now, I can see that as much as I wish I could tell Billy that things are going to be all right, *he* is in fact the one who is telling me that. His story inspires me to this day to be a better man, to be a better husband, and to try harder to walk the right path, even when times are dark and uncertain.

He tells me to get back to writing this book because this story can help people even if it hurts to do it.

Just like your life story is still being written, even though it may hurt at times, remember: pain can be an excellent teacher.

Since I can't go back and tell myself that it's going to be okay, the best thing I can do is tell you that it's going to be okay. That there is darkness in the world but there is also light, and there is always the opportunity to redefine what this moment—what any moment—means to you.

I'm not blind to the realities of the world. Bad things happen to good people. People die far too young. People do horrible things to others—sometimes to you and me. We need time to grieve. To process.

But if we are to keep moving forward as individuals, as families, as a species, we need to realize and act on the power we have to define our reality. We can't control everything, but we can guide and choose the meaning for our situations. In that way, we can make real progress.

That is what this book is about. It's about your story and my story and Daniele's story—it's about all our stories.

Stories are told to pass on lessons, to inspire, to connect and bond, and bring us closer together.

Young Billy's story is about a brave and bold boy who grew into the man typing this today.

I can't go back in time and tell him it will be okay, but I can promise him that I will tell his story so that he can inspire others to be brave and look inward for the answers.

I can tell my parents that it turned out well thanks to their love in uncertain times. I can tell my brother that through our actions and missteps as younger versions of ourselves, we now have the opportunity to help so many, and that the time for forgiveness is now.

And I can tell you that if you're reading this, you are reading it for a reason. It's up to you to decide what that reason is that guided you here, to this book, in this moment.

I remember the critical moment when I was 34 years old, coughing up dust under the basement stairs as I re-discovered the *Chronicles of the Warrior Lost*:

I began to get an understanding of what was going on. Why billions of dollars were being spent on this project. The weird part is I was not raised with compassion. I learned what they wanted me to learn and yet with the constant brainwashing I still had my own thoughts and feelings.

I will never understand how that happened. It just did...

I now understand why I did have compassion. Because of love, forgiveness, a never-give-up attitude, and not letting other people dictate how I should be, act, or feel.

The same goodness I have inside me is the same goodness you have inside of you. That same spark of goodness is in everyone.

I'm no longer the Warrior Lost for I have found my purpose. I am a Next Level Life Warrior that fights to make a better life for myself, my family, friends, and all the inhabitants of this planet, including those like you, who are ready to take their next step to a better life.

Daniele and I can only point the finger in the direction of our truth and success, just like so many that have come before us have shared their versions of their truths by pointing toward the path.

It's up to you to discover your truth for yourself.

It's up to you to take new, empowering actions, and adopt them as *practices*, especially when they bring you joy.

It's up to you to take the next step.

We hope that you have learned something here and will choose to take a new action or two (or more if you're up for it).

And we hope that you will love more, be more forgiving, and never, ever give up, because you deserve to live a life that is full of the joys these *practices* bring to you and those you care about.

It's up to you to decide whether or not to take action, to discover your own truth, to turn adversity into advantage, to turn tragedy into triumph, and to live your life at the next level.

What will you decide?

YOUR NEXT LEVEL LIFE STORY

"The nitrogen in our DNA, the calcium in our teeth, the iron in our blood, the carbon in our apple pies were made in the interiors of collapsing stars. We are made of star-stuff."
— Carl Sagan

The reality is this: This is *your* life. Not your parents' life, not your children's life, not your friend's life, not your partner's life. This is your life to choose how to live. Through the actions you take you are directly writing your Next Level Life Story.

Just by reading this book and (hopefully) others like it, you are opening yourself up to consciously choosing your path. Remember that raft in the beginning? The one that was being thrown around at the whims of the sea and the storms?

By reading this book you have essentially transformed that raft into the sailboat we spoke of, and now you must *practice* steering and using the wind—the powers of nature, the ups and downs of life—to guide you along the way.

It's up to you to start from wherever you are currently standing—whether it's at the bottom of a pit of despair or at the top of a peak of success, there always has been and always will be a next level to aspire to reach. That's the human condition, the Earth condition, the cosmic condition, the DNA-level, uncontrollable urge to evolve.

It's a never-ending quest. It can be inspiring and it can be daunting.

It's like what happens when we observe the size of ourselves and our home planet in comparison to the Universe as a whole. Our planet orbits our sun that is just one of more than ten-sextillion other stars in the Universe. That's a 1 followed by 22 zeros, and it's more stars than there are grains of sand on every beach on Earth!

There's a reddish star that is often visible by the naked eye in the Northern Hemisphere from late spring to early winter in the night sky called Antares. Antares is ten thousand times brighter than our own sun, and if it were in the center of our solar system, its surface would reach out beyond Mars!

It brings to mind Carl Sagan's quote, "Science is not only compatible with spirituality; it is a profound source of spirituality."

The message we get from science and spirituality is that it's an unfathomably extraordinary opportunity to simply be alive at all, let alone in this time, in this day and age. When someone was diagnosed with type 1 diabetes prior to 1921, the only option they had was death as a treatment wasn't yet discovered. Pure gratitude abounds every single day for the miracle of life we have been given.

We all have the gift and responsibility of awareness and choice. The gift of the knowledge of our place in the Universe, and the choice of whether we allow that to scare us or inspire us or both—as long as that fear and inspiration leads to courageous, conscious action.

We have choices in life every single moment of every single day. Every choice matters. If and when this realization feels daunting, always remember: don't allow your blessings to feel like burdens.

Never stop learning, growing, and striving to make the most of yourself and the unlimited potential you have in this world.

The concept of unrealized potential is a real and intimidating one. Whether your goal is to change the life of a billion people, or just one person dear to you, or just yourself, we are all in this together regardless.

We both love this little word scramble puzzle and hope that it helps you remember to intentionally find and create joy throughout as you travel your path: enjoy + ur = journey

Enjoy your journey—it's your choice. Find a way to laugh or to make someone else laugh. Smile at strangers. Pet animals. Hug people. Hug trees. Stand barefoot in the grass, on the sand, or in the dirt. Let your Love Sun shine!

There are unlimited places you can go from here. Amazing places to see, people to meet, cultures to experience, nature to explore, and ways of life to examine, and it starts with you making a decision that you are worthy of experiencing these things.

In case you still weren't sure, let us assure you: you are worthy of all the good things life has to offer—and in abundance.

A TV show, movie, book, or video game might give you good feelings or a positive message, but it's up to you to carry your own message—your own truth—forward. It is up to you to decide what the meaning of your life is, how you want to feel, and how you want to make others feel, and then get to work on carrying that message forward into your actions as often as possible.

It's up to you to choose the meanings you give to your life and whether those meanings have the potential to help others along the way.

That's what living a Next Level Life is all about.

And if you stop to think about it, you'll realize that you've already begun to live your life this way.

And now it's about being more conscious and purposeful in your actions and interactions with others.

"If one advances confidently in the direction of his dreams, and endeavors to live the life which he has imagined, he will meet with a success unexpected in common hours."
— Henry David Thoreau

Know in your heart that you will continue to be guided on your journey, and remember, even though we may have never met you (though it feels like we have), we believe in you. We love you.

And always remember that in any moment you can choose to love strong, be forgiving, and never, ever give up on being your best self.

Let's join forces and choose to be more loving—both toward ourselves and others—because you deserve it and the world needs as much love as it can get!

HERO'S QUEST: YOU ARE VICTORIOUS

"Do. Or do not. There is no try."
—Yoda, *The Empire Strikes Back*

One final note on heroes in stories. Once the hero has vanquished the villain, both external and internal, they are forever changed. That doesn't mean further challenges won't arise. They will. But now you'll be prepared to handle those challenges.

The hero returns to their village with the prize, the knowledge, the treasure, and shares it with those they care about. They give to others what they have been gifted. We hope you'll do the same with any knowledge and experience you have gained on your quest.

Be sure to keep a watchful eye for new companions and powerful allies to accompany you on your future adventures.

If this book—this magical tome—was helpful to you, can you think of just one other person who would benefit from it?

If so, kindly consider gifting them a copy so they can go on their own epic journey.

Always remember, you have on you at all times your Shield of Love, Orb of Forgiveness, and Sword of Perseverance.

Wield them wisely and justly on your journey.

Read on to receive your final gift...

AFTERWORD

And a SPECIAL OFFER for the first 100 readers to get Book 2 for FREE:

Thank you for reading *Love, Forgive, Never Give Up! Book 1*. I hope you enjoyed reading it as much as we enjoyed writing it.

As authors, we love discovering readers that *really* enjoy reading our books.

So if you really like Book 1 and you leave us a review, we'll send you Book 2 for free!

Here are the steps:
Step 1: First, leave a review on the book page here: www.LFNBookReview.com
Step 2: Then, send us an email at review@LFNBook.com letting us know you posted a review and where to find it (screenshot, forward your review confirmation, etc.)
Step 3: After steps 1 and 2 are complete, we'll send you a digital copy of Book 2 to read for free as soon as it becomes available.
It's that simple!

We love hearing from our readers regarding their thoughts on the book and how their lives have been impacted. If you have a story to share, send an email to MyStory@LFNBook.com

Thank you so much for reading and sharing your thoughts. We're hard at work on Book 2 where we'll continue with 33 more lessons on taking your life to the next level through love, forgiveness, and never giving up!

Sign up for updates on Book 2 and beyond at: www.LFNBook.com

With gratitude, Bill and Daniele Hargenrader

ACKNOWLEDGMENTS

Our hearts are filled with deep love and gratitude for everyone who has helped us along the way. Many more people have contributed to the evolution of this book then we can thank here.

We would like to thank our families, including our close and distant relatives, and our ancestors for passing on their knowledge and giving the gift of life. Thank you to Daniele's mom, Gayle Shapiro, for always being there and reading early drafts along the way. Special thanks to Bill's mom, dad, and brother: please remember that forgiveness is a gift we can choose to give ourselves.

Many thanks to our friends we've met along the way: Alexis Kurtz, Samara O'Shea, Aaron Rushing, Rob Rosell, Irene Sagalovsky, Scott Bick, Ben and Annie Warrene, Shawn Glass, Kip Brooks, Asha Brown, Jody Stanislaw, Barry Fritz, Alex Papanikalou, Kurt Black, Shaylyn Leahy, Michael and Roslyn Rozbruch, Michael Daszczuk, Julie Jacky, Kim Julen, Brent Seal, Kathleen and Robert Starmer, Tom and Gina Scarda, Allan Ting, Miguel Cavalcanti, Paula Abreu, Dragan Trajkovski, Andy Zittzmann, April Sumner, Brian Adams, Chris York, Mimi Jones, David Beaudry, Ron Sparkman, and so many more!

Big thanks to our Editors and Proofreaders, Corey McCollough and Sheenah Freitas, as well as Rick Frishman, Scott Frishman, and the team behind the scenes at Author 101.

A huge thank you to our mentors and influencers Tony Robbins, Julia Cameron, Brendon Burchard, Bo Eason, Jack Canfield, Marianne Williamson, Brian Tracy, Tim Ferriss, Deepak Chopra, Oprah Winfrey, Gabrielle Bernstein, Stephen King, Steven Pressfield, James Redfield, Preston Smiles, Eckhart Tolle, the late greats: Napoleon Hill, Wayne Dyer, Viktor Frankl, Florence Scovel Shinn, and so many that have come before us and taken the time to share their wisdom and life experience.

"To Daniele, my wife, my all, my everything. You inspire every day to reaffirm my commitment not only to you, but to our shared vision that is much like the lighthouse where we got married, our mission to blaze bright and strong, living our lives to our fullest, to be a light of hope to those in dark places, and to be a shining example of what is possible in this world." — Bill

"Without Bill's unconditional and unwavering love, support, encouragement, and belief in my true goddess-nature over the past eleven years, I would not have had the privilege of understanding the ever-growing, infinite, Earth-shattering, profound depths of true love and equal partnership. As Fabolous + Ne-Yo said: 'I'm a movement by myself, but I'm a force when we're together... you make me better.'" —Daniele

And most of all, we want to thank our readers that are stepping up and taking action to make their lives, communities, and the world a kinder, more loving place to live in. The light in us recognizes and honors the light in you. *Namaste*. Thank you!

CROWDFUNDING THANK YOU PAGE

These extraordinary humans pledged to support our Kickstarter campaign at a significant level. Thank you for believing in our vision from the start!

Here are the backers for our 10X Value Level in the order of pledge received, first to final:

- Elizabeth Petersen
- Michael Rozbruch
- Julie Jacky
- Tom Scarda
- Karyn Folan
- Lucy Hoger
- Aaron Rushing
- Mike Durbin

"The work that both of you do has an amazing impact on everyone around you. Daniele is my Diabetes Coach and a great friend, and I highly respect the work of both her and Bill!"
—Elizabeth Petersen

Thank you to everyone who supported our book!

Your belief and faith in us has motivated and inspired us more than you know.

ALSO BY THE AUTHORS

By Daniele Hargenrader: *Unleash Your Inner Diabetes Dominator: How to Use Your Powers of Choice, Self-Love, and Community to Completely Change Your Relationship with Diabetes for the Better*

Unleash Your Inner Diabetes Dominator is an interactive guidebook with an easy-to-follow, repeatedly-proven system filled with inspiring stories showing you how to claim your personal power written for people with diabetes and our loved ones.

After reading this book, you can expect to feel a paradigm shift in the way you look at diabetes, an increased confidence in yourself and your capacity to handle any challenges you are faced with, as well as feelings of empowerment, pride, and accomplishment as you move from surviving to thriving.

3 BONUSES: Get one of Daniele's best online health and wellness training programs for FREE (over $100 Value) when you take action now and go to: www.diabetesbook.com

By Bill Hargenrader: *The Mars Journey Series*
Mars Journey: Call to Action: Book 1 is the first book in the bestselling epic science fiction, action and adventure thriller series set in the near future:

Brent Carlson, a brilliant but disgraced former astronaut, embarks on a modern day quest to gather and train the crew of the first international mission to Mars. Meanwhile, the power-hungry billionaire CEO of a massive global technology conglomerate has launched a bid to reach Mars first and claim the red planet as corporate property.

For a limited time: Get the first book in the series for free at: www.FreeMarsBook.com

ABOUT THE AUTHORS

Bill Hargenrader is an international speaker, a United States Army Veteran, a Fortune 500 Project Management Professional focusing on cybersecurity and innovation, a proactive Humans to Mars advocate, and founder of Next Level Life, where he focuses on empowering entrepreneurs and artists so we can massively change the world for the better together.

When Bill was 8 years old he was wrongfully committed to a mental institution for 3 years due to an unfortunate course of events. This set him on a lifelong quest of learning and discovery to figure out what the best tools are for us to truly change our lives for the better. Now Bill is a bestselling author of the Mars Journey series and an international keynote speaker who is both a technical presenter and an inspirational motivator with his talks ranging from the latest advances in technology to advancing through our lives realizing that we can be the hero of our own story.

Get timely updates on Bill's books and other projects at www.billhargenrader.com

Daniele Hargenrader is the bestselling author of *Unleash Your Inner Diabetes Dominator* and founder of Diabetes Dominator Coaching. She is a nutritionist, diabetes, health + life coach, and certified personal trainer, and has been living with type 1 diabetes since 1991. Daniele founded Diabetes Dominator Coaching in 2009 with the intention of serving those who are looking for a path to turn a perceived adversity into an advantage through her Six Pillars of Total Health system. She helps individuals from all walks of life to think, eat, and move in ways that allow them to achieve a quality of health and life that they previously thought unattainable.

She is a professional international speaker and corporate consultant, has presented at Fortune 500 companies and top-ranked hospitals and universities, and has dedicated herself to teaching people how to live the life they imagined. Daniele ballooned up to 200 pounds a few years after her diagnosis and suffered from the unexpected and sudden death of her father while battling clinical depression and a binge-eating addiction. Through these adversities, she eventually took herself from obese to athlete and from suffering to flourishing.

Daniele currently lives in Philadelphia with her husband, Bill, and their two cats, Kitty and Frankie. Meet Daniele and receive free training and resources at www.DiabetesDominator.com.

Made in the USA
Lexington, KY
26 October 2019

55915258R00114